MICROSOFT Windows 98
Essential Concepts and Techniques

Gary B. Shelly
Thomas J. Cashman
Steven G. Forsythe

COURSE TECHNOLOGY
ONE MAIN STREET
CAMBRIDGE MA 02142

an International Thomson Publishing company

SHELLY
CASHMAN
SERIES.

CAMBRIDGE • ALBANY • BONN • CINCINNATI • LONDON • MADRID • MELBOURNE

MEXICO CITY • NEW YORK • PARIS • SAN FRANCISCO • TOKYO • TORONTO • WASHINGTON

COURSE
TECHNOLOGY

MICROSOFT
Windows 98
Essential Concepts and Techniques

C O N T E N T S

Preface

The Shelly Cashman Series® offers the finest textbooks in computer education. The Microsoft Windows 98 books continue with the innovation, quality, and reliability consistent with this series. We are proud that both our Microsoft Windows 3.1 and Microsoft Windows 95 books were used by more schools and more students than any other series in textbook publishing.

The Windows 98 interface includes a new Quick Launch toolbar on the taskbar, additional toolbars you can add to the taskbar, and a choice of three desktop views (Web style, Classic style, and Custom style). The Web style turns on the Active Desktop™ that places the Internet Explorer Channel bar and constantly changing Web content on the desktop, lets you point to an icon to select it and single-click the icon to open its window, and displays folders that look and respond like Web pages.

In our Microsoft Windows 98 books, you will find an educationally sound and easy-to-follow pedagogy that combines a step-by-step approach with corresponding screens. The Other Ways and More About features offer in-depth knowledge of Windows 98. The all-new project openers provide a fascinating perspective on the subject covered in the project. The Shelly Cashman Series Microsoft Windows 98 textbooks will make your computer applications class exciting and dynamic and one that your students will remember as one of their better educational experiences.

Objectives of This Textbook

Microsoft Windows 98: Essential Concepts and Techniques is intended for use in combination with other books in an introduction to computers or computer applications course. No computer experience is assumed. The objectives of this book are:

- To teach the fundamentals and skills necessary to adequately use Windows 98
- To provide a knowledge base for Windows 98 upon which students can build
- To expose students to real-world examples and procedures that will prepare them to be skilled users of Windows 98
- To encourage independent study and help those who are working alone in a distance education environment

When students complete the course using this textbook, they will have a basic knowledge and understanding of Windows 98.

The Shelly Cashman Approach

Features of the Shelly Cashman Series Microsoft Windows 98 books include:

- **Project Orientation:** Related topics are presented using a project orientation that establishes a strong foundation on which students can confidently learn more advanced topics.
- **Screen-by-Screen, Step-by-Step Instructions:** Each task required to complete a project is identified throughout the development of the project. Then, steps to accomplish the task are specified and are accompanied by screens.
- **Thoroughly Tested Projects:** Every screen in the textbook is correct because it is produced by the author only after performing a step, which results in unprecedented quality.
- **Two-Page Project Openers:** Each project begins with a two-page opener that sets the tone for the project by describing an interesting aspect of Windows 98.
- **Other Ways Boxes for Reference:** Microsoft Windows 98 provides a variety of ways to carry out a given task. The Other Ways boxes displayed at the end of most of the step-by-step sequences specify the other ways to do the task completed in the steps. Thus, the steps and the Other Ways box make a comprehensive reference unit.
- **More About Feature:** These marginal annotations provide background information about the topics covered, adding interest and depth to learning.

Other Ways

1. To select contiguous files, select first file name, hold down SHIFT key, click last file name
2. To select all files, on Edit menu click Select All

More About

The Windows 98 Interface

The Windows 98 graphical user interface is similar to and an improvement of the Windows 95 graphical user interface. Thousands of hours were spent making improvements to Windows 95. Of tremendous importance were Microsoft's usability labs, where everyone from raw beginners to experts interacted with many different versions of the interface. The Quick Launch toolbar and other significant improvements of the Windows 98 interface emerged from the experiences in these labs.

Organization of This Textbook

Microsoft Windows 98: Essential Concepts and Techniques consists of two projects, as follows:

Project 1 - Fundamentals of Using Microsoft Windows 98   In Project 1, students learn about user interfaces and Microsoft Windows 98. Topics include launching Microsoft Windows 98; mouse operations; maximizing and minimizing windows; sizing and scrolling windows; describing the Internet and World Wide Web; recognizing the Classic style, Web style, and Custom style; launching an application program; using Windows Help; and shutting down Windows 98.

Project 2 - Using Windows Explorer   In Project 2, students are introduced to Windows Explorer. Topics include displaying the contents of a folder; expanding and collapsing a folder; changing the view; selecting and copying a group of files; creating, renaming, and deleting a folder; and renaming and deleting a file.

End-of-Project Student Activities

A notable strength of the Shelly Cashman Series Microsoft Windows 98 textbooks is the extensive student activities at the end of each project. Well-structured student activities can make the difference between students merely participating in a class and students retaining the information they learn. These activities include:

- **What You Should Know** A listing of the tasks completed within a project together with the pages where the step-by-step, screen-by-screen explanations appear. This section provides a perfect study review for students.

- **Test Your Knowledge** Four activities designed to determine students' understanding of the material in the project. Included are true/false questions, multiple-choice questions, and two other unique activities.

- **Use Help** Users of Windows 98 must know how to use Help. This book contains extensive Help activities. These exercises alone distinguish the Shelly Cashman Series from any other set of Windows 98 instructional materials.

- **In the Lab** These assignments require students to make use of the knowledge gained in the project to solve problems on a computer.

- **Cases and Places** Unique case studies allow students to apply their knowledge to real-world situations. These case studies provide subjects for research papers based on information gained from a resource such as the Internet.

Instructor's Resource Kit

A comprehensive Instructor's Resource Kit (IRK) accompanies this book in the form of a CD-ROM. The CD-ROM includes the Instructor's Manual and other teaching and testing aids. The CD-ROM (ISBN 0-7895-4301-x) is available through your Course Technology representative. The contents of the CD-ROM follow.

- **Instructor's Manual** The Instructor's Manual is made up of Microsoft Word files that include lecture notes, solutions to laboratory assignments, and a large test bank. The files allow you to modify the lecture notes or generate quizzes and exams from the test bank using your own word processor. Where appropriate, solutions to laboratory assignments are embedded as icons in the files.

- **Figures in the Book** Illustrations for every screen in the textbook are available. Use this ancillary to create a slide show from the illustrations for lecture or to print transparencies for use in lecture with an overhead projector.

- **Course Test Manager** Course Test Manager is a powerful testing and assessment package that enables instructors to create and print tests from the large test bank. Instructors with access to a networked computer lab (LAN) can administer, grade, and track tests online.

- **Interactive Labs** Eighteen hands-on interactive labs solidify and reinforce computer concepts.

Shelly Cashman Online

Shelly Cashman Online is a World Wide Web service available to instructors and students of computer education. Visit Shelly Cashman Online at www.scseries.com. Shelly Cashman Online is divided into four areas:

- **Series Information** Information on the Shelly Cashman Series products.
- **Teaching Resources** Designed for instructors teaching from and using Shelly Cashman Series textbooks and software. This area includes password-protected instructor materials that can be downloaded, course outlines, teaching and tips, and much more.
- **Student Center** Dedicated to students learning about computers with Shelly Cashman Series textbooks and software. This area includes cool links, data that can be downloaded, and much more.
- **Community** Opportunities to discuss your course and your ideas with instructors in your field and with the Shelly Cashman Series team.

Acknowledgments

The Shelly Cashman Series would not be the leading computer education series without the contributions of outstanding publishing professionals. First and foremost among them is Becky Herrington, director of production and designer. She is the heart and soul of the Shelly Cashman Series, and it is only through her leadership, dedication, and tireless efforts that superior products are made possible.

Under Becky's direction, the following individuals made significant contributions to these books: Doug Cowley, production manager; Ginny Harvey, series specialist and developmental editor; Ken Russo, graphic designer and Web developer; Mike Bodnar, Stephanie Nance, Dave Bonnewitz, and Mark Norton, graphic artists; Jeanne Black, Quark expert; Marilyn Martin, proofreader; Marlo Mitchem, administrative/production assistant; Cristina Haley, indexer; Sarah Evertson of Image Quest, photo researcher; and Susan Sebok contributing writer.

Special thanks go to Jim Quasney, our dedicated series editor; Lisa Strite, senior editor; Lora Wade, associate product manager; Tonia Grafakos and Meagan Walsh, editorial assistants; and Kathryn Coyne, product marketing manager. Special mention must go to Becky Herrington for the outstanding book design, Mike Bodnar for the logo designs, and Ken Russo for the cover design and illustrations.

Gary B. Shelly
Thomas J. Cashman
Steven G. Forsythe

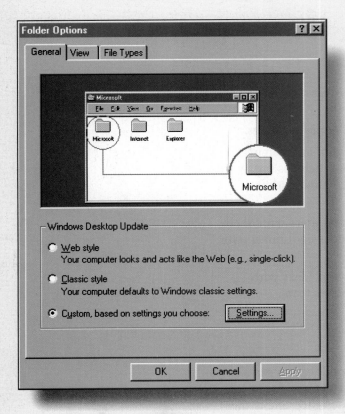

FIGURE 1a

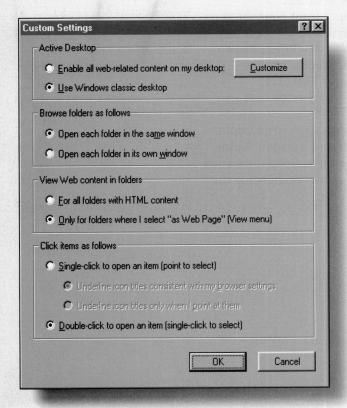

FIGURE 1b

Instructions for Selecting the Default Desktop View Settings

The projects and assignments in this textbook are presented using the default desktop view settings (default Custom style), as chosen by Microsoft Corporation. With the exception of the Open each folder in the same window option, the default settings are those of the Classic style. To ensure your success in completing the projects and assignments, the Windows 98 operating system must be installed on your computer system and the default desktop view settings must be selected. The following steps illustrate how to use the Folder Options dialog box and Custom Settings dialog box to select the default settings.

1. Click the Start button on the taskbar.
2. Point to Settings on the Start menu.
3. Click Folder Options on the Settings submenu to display the Folder Options dialog box (Figure 1a).
4. If necessary, click the General tab in the Folder Options dialog box to display the General sheet.
5. If necessary, click Custom, based on settings you choose to select the option.
6. Click the Settings button in the Folder Options dialog box to open the Custom Settings dialog box (Figure 1b).
7. On a piece of paper, write down the name of each option button that is selected in the Custom Settings dialog box.
8. Click Use Windows classic desktop to select the option.
9. Click Open each folder in the same window to select the option.
10. Click Only for folders where I select "as Web Page" (View menu) to select the option.
11. Click Double-click to open an item (single-click to select) to select the option.
12. Click the OK button in the Custom Settings dialog box.
13. Click the Close button in the Folder Options dialog box.

As a result of selecting the default settings, you can perform the steps and assignments in each project of this book. If, after finishing the steps and assignments, you must reset the desktop view to its original settings, perform steps 1 through 6 above, click the option button of each setting you wrote down in step 7, and then perform steps 12 and 13.

Microsoft Windows 98

P R O J E C T

1

Microsoft Windows 98

Fundamentals of Using Microsoft Windows 98

You will have mastered the material in this project when you can:

O B J E C T I V E S

- Describe Microsoft Windows 98
- Explain a user interface
- Identify the objects on the Microsoft Windows 98 desktop
- Perform the basic mouse operations: point, click, right-click, double-click, drag, and right-drag
- Open, minimize, maximize, restore, and close a window
- Move and resize a window on the Windows 98 desktop
- Scroll in a window
- Understand keyboard shortcut notation
- Identify the three desktop views: Classic style, Web style, and Custom style
- Describe the Internet and World Wide Web
- Launch an application program
- Use Windows 98 Help
- Shut down Windows 98

The Best Job In The Whole World

Bill Gates Uses His Leave Wisely

"My job probably is the best job in the whole world." No wonder Bill Gates makes this claim: as founder and CEO of Microsoft, he is the richest person on the planet with a net worth estimated at $50 billion—not bad for a Harvard College student "on leave."

His computing efforts began in grade school when he and a classmate, Paul Allen, learned the BASIC programming language from a manual and programmed a mainframe computer using a Teletype terminal purchased with proceeds from a rummage sale. In 1968, they wrote a program to play tic-tac-toe. Then they developed more complex programs, including one resembling the board game Risk with the objective of world dominance.

In high school, Gates and Allen had a thirst for more computing power than the Teletype terminal could offer. They wrote custom programs for local

businesses during the summer and split their $5,000 salaries between cash and computer time, which cost them about $40 per hour. In addition, they debugged software problems at local businesses in return for computer use. In Gates's sophomore year, one of his teachers asked him to teach his computer skills to his classmates. Also, he boasts that he wrote a program to schedule students in classes and changed a few lines of code so he was the only male in a class full of females.

When Gates was 16 in 1972, he and Allen read a ten-paragraph article in *Electronics* magazine about Intel's first microprocessor chip. They requested a manual from Intel, experimented with pushing the chip to its limits, and formed the Traf-O-Data company. This pursuit involved developing a device about the size of a toaster oven with a rubber hose connected to a metal box containing a paper tape. When a car ran over the hose, the device punched a hole in the tape. They used the Intel chip to analyze the tape and subsequently to determine traffic flow in several cities.

Gates entered Harvard College in 1973, and Allen landed a job programming Honeywell mini-computers in Boston. They continued to scheme about the power of computers. In Gates's sophomore year, they saw a picture of the Altair 8800 computer on the cover of the January 1975 edition of *Popular Electronics*. That computer was about the size of the Traf-O-Data device and contained a new Intel computer chip. For five weeks, they spent sleepless nights writing BASIC for that computer, and Gates says that on some of those days, he did not see anyone or eat.

At that point they formed the world's first micro-computer software company: Microsoft Corporation. They realized they needed to make some sacrifices to achieve their goal of "a computer on every desk and in every home," so Allen quit his job and Gates left Harvard. Gates says he always planned to return to earn his degree, and he considers himself "on a really long leave." In the interim, he has added 25,000 employees to help him achieve yearly net revenues surpassing $11 billion.

Microsoft Windows 98

Fundamentals of Using Microsoft Windows 98

P R O J E C T

1

C A S E P E R S P E C T I V E

Everyday from locations around the world, millions of Windows 98 users turn on their computers. When the computer starts, the first image on the monitor is the Windows 98 desktop. If these users did not know how to launch an application program, manipulate files and objects on the desktop, send and receive e-mail, and obtain information using the Internet and/or intranet, their computers would be useless.

You have just acquired a computer with the Windows 98 operating system. Your task is to learn the basics of Windows 98 so your computer will be useful to you, and you will be able to assist others who may come to you with questions and requests.

Introduction

An **operating system** is the set of computer instructions, called a computer program, that controls the allocation of computer hardware such as memory, disk devices, printers, and CD-ROM and DVD drives, and provides the capability for you to communicate with your computer. The most popular and widely used operating system for personal computers is **Microsoft Windows**. **Microsoft Windows 98** (called **Windows 98** for the rest of this book), the newest version of Microsoft Windows, allows you easily to communicate with and control your computer.

Windows 98 is easy to use and can be customized to fit individual needs. Windows 98 simplifies the process of working with documents and applications, transferring data between documents, organizing the manner in which you interact with your computer, and using your computer to access information on the Internet and/or intranet. In Project 1, you will learn about Windows 98 and how to use the Windows 98 user interface.

Microsoft Windows 98

Microsoft Windows 98 is an operating system that performs every function necessary for you to communicate with and use your computer. Windows 98 is called a **32-bit operating system** because it uses 32 bits for addressing and other purposes, which means the operating system can address more than four gigabytes of RAM (random-access memory) and perform tasks faster than older operating systems. Windows 98 includes **Microsoft Internet Explorer (IE)**, a software program developed by Microsoft Corporation, that integrates the Windows 98 desktop and the Internet. Internet Explorer allows you to work with programs and files in a similar fashion, whether they are located on your computer, a local network, or the Internet.

Windows 98 is designed to be compatible with all existing **application programs**, which are programs that perform an application-related function such as word processing. To use the application programs that can be executed under Windows 98, you must know about the Windows 98 user interface.

What Is a User Interface?

A **user interface** is the combination of hardware and software that you use to communicate with and control your computer. Through the user interface, you are able to make selections on your computer, request information from your computer, and respond to messages displayed by your computer. Thus, a user interface provides the means for dialogue between you and your computer.

Hardware and software together form the user interface. Among the hardware devices associated with a user interface are the monitor, keyboard, and mouse (Figure 1-1). The **monitor** displays messages and provides information. You respond by entering data in the form of a command or other response using the **keyboard** or **mouse**. Among the responses available to you are responses that specify what application program to run, what document to open, when to print, and where to store data for future use.

The computer software associated with the user interface consists of the programs that engage you in dialogue (Figure 1-1). The computer software determines the messages you receive, the manner in which you should respond, and the actions that occur based on your responses.

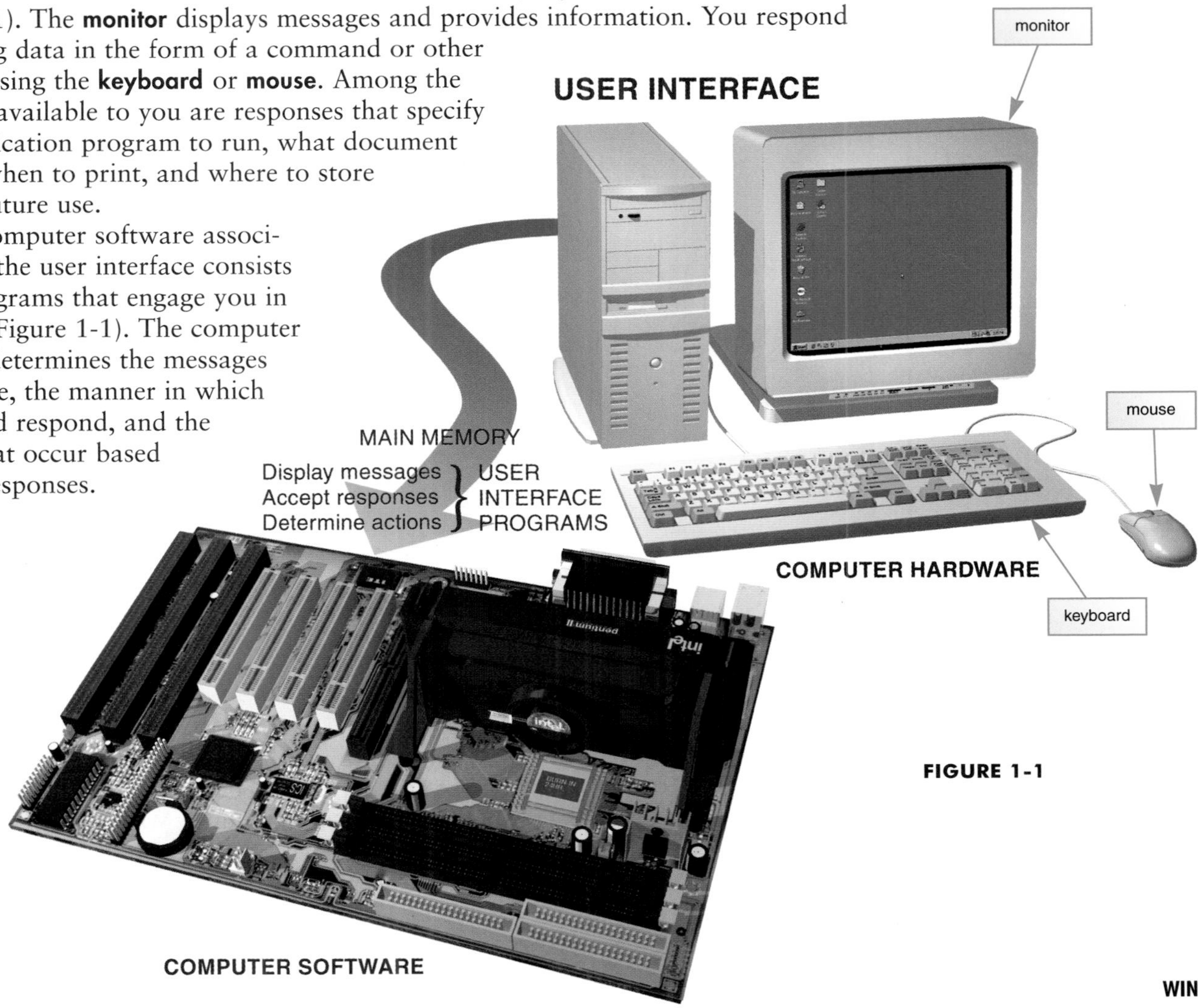

USER INTERFACE

monitor

MAIN MEMORY

Display messages ⎫ USER
Accept responses ⎬ INTERFACE
Determine actions ⎭ PROGRAMS

mouse

COMPUTER HARDWARE

keyboard

FIGURE 1-1

COMPUTER SOFTWARE

More *About*

The Windows 98 Interface

The Windows 98 graphical user interface is similar to and an improvement of the Windows 95 graphical user interface. Thousands of hours were spent making improvements to Windows 95. Of tremendous importance were Microsoft's usability labs, where everyone from raw beginners to experts interacted with many different versions of the interface. The Quick Launch toolbar and other significant improvements of the Windows 98 interface emerged from the experiences in these labs.

The goal of an effective user interface is to be **user friendly**, meaning that the software can be used easily by individuals with limited training. Research studies have indicated that the use of graphics can play an important role in aiding users to interact effectively with a computer. A **graphical user interface**, or **GUI** (pronounced gooey), is a user interface that displays graphics in addition to text when it communicates with the user.

The Windows 98 graphical user interface was carefully designed to be easier to set up, simpler to learn, faster and more powerful, and better integrated with the Internet than previous versions of Microsoft Windows.

Launching Microsoft Windows 98

When you turn on your computer, an introductory screen consisting of the Windows logo and Windows 98 name displays on a blue sky and clouds background in the middle of the screen. The screen clears and several items display on a background called the **desktop.** The default color of the desktop background is green, but your computer may display a different color. Your screen will display as shown in Figure 1-2. It may also display without the Welcome screen shown in Figure 1-2.

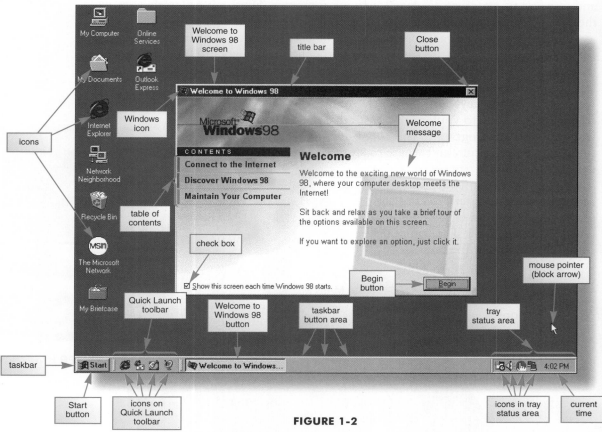

FIGURE 1-2

The items on the desktop shown in Figure 1-2 include nine icons and their titles on the left side of the desktop and the taskbar at the bottom of the desktop. Using the nine **icons**, you can view the contents of your computer (**My Computer**), store documents in one location (**My Documents**), connect to and browse the Internet (**Internet Explorer**), work with other computers connected to your computer (**Network Neighborhood**), discard unneeded objects (**Recycle Bin**), connect to the Microsoft Network online service (**The Microsoft Network**), transfer documents or folders to and from a portable computer (**My Briefcase**), investigate other online services (**Online Services**), and receive and send e-mail (**Outlook Express**). Your computer's desktop might contain more, fewer, or some different icons because the desktop of the computer can be customized.

The **taskbar** at the bottom of the screen in Figure 1-2 contains the Start button, Quick Launch toolbar, taskbar button area, and the tray status area. The **Start button** allows you to launch a program quickly, find or open a document, change your computer's settings, shut down the computer, and perform many more tasks. The **Quick Launch toolbar** contains four icons that allow you to launch Internet Explorer (**Launch Internet Explorer Browser**), launch Outlook Express (**Launch Outlook Express**), view an uncluttered desktop at any time (**Show Desktop**), and view a list of channels (**View Channels**).

The **taskbar button area** contains buttons to indicate which windows are open on the desktop. In Figure 1-2, the Welcome to Windows 98 screen displays on the desktop and the Welcome to Windows 98 button displays in the taskbar button area. The **tray status area** contains the **Task Scheduler icon** to schedule daily tasks, a **speaker icon** to adjust the computer's volume level, **The Microsoft Network icon** to connect to The Microsoft Network online service, the **Internet connection icon** to indicate a modem is being used to connect to the Internet, and the current time (4:02 PM). The tray status area on your desktop might contain more, fewer, or some different icons because the contents of the tray status area can be changed.

The Welcome to Windows 98 screen that may display on your desktop when you launch Windows 98 is shown in Figure 1-2. The **title bar**, which is dark blue in color at the top of the screen, contains the Windows icon, identifies the name of the screen (Welcome to Windows 98), and contains the Close button, which can be used to close the Welcome to Windows 98 screen.

On the Welcome to Windows 98 screen, a table of contents contains three options (Connect to the Internet, Discover Windows 98, and Maintain Your Computer). The options in the table of contents allow you to perform different tasks such as connecting to the Internet, learning Windows 98 using the Discover Windows 98 tutorial, and improving the performance of your computer. A welcome message (Welcome) to the right of the table of contents welcomes you to the world of Windows 98. Pointing to an option in the table of contents replaces the Welcome message with an explanation of the option. The **Begin button** in the lower-right corner begins the process of connecting to the Internet, and a check mark in the **check box** to the left of the Begin button indicates the Welcome to Windows 98 screen will display each time you start Windows 98.

In the lower-right corner of the screen is the mouse pointer. On the desktop, the **mouse pointer** is the shape of a block arrow. The mouse pointer allows you to point to objects on the desktop and may change shape when it points to different objects.

Nearly every item on the Windows 98 desktop is considered an object. Even the desktop itself is an object. Every **object** has properties. The **properties** of an object are unique to that specific object and may affect what can be done to the object or what the object does. For example, the properties of an object may be the color of the object, such as the color of the desktop.

Closing the Welcome Screen

As noted, the Welcome screen may display when you launch Windows 98. If the Welcome screen does display on the desktop, normally you should close it prior to beginning any other operations using Windows 98. To close the Welcome screen, complete the step on the next page.

The Windows 98 Desktop

Because Windows 98 is easily customized, the desktop on your computer may not resemble the desktop in Figure 1-2. For example, the icon titles on the desktop may be underlined or objects not shown in Figure 1-2 may display on your desktop. If this is the case, refer to page viii of the Preface of this book for instructions for selecting the default desktop view settings or contact your instructor to change the desktop view.

TO CLOSE THE WELCOME SCREEN

① Press and hold the ALT key on the keyboard and then press the F4 key on the keyboard. Release the ALT key.

The Welcome to Windows 98 screen closes.

The Desktop as a Work Area

The Windows 98 desktop and the objects on the desktop were designed to emulate a work area in an office or at home. The Windows desktop may be thought of as an electronic version of the top of your desk. You can move objects around on the desktop, look at them and then put them aside, and so on. In Project 1, you will learn how to interact with and communicate with the Windows 98 desktop.

Communicating with Microsoft Windows 98

The Windows 98 interface provides the means for dialogue between you and your computer. Part of this dialogue involves your requesting information from your computer and responding to messages displayed by your computer. You can request information and respond to messages using either a mouse or a keyboard.

Mouse Operations

A **mouse** is a pointing device used with Windows 98 that is attached to the computer by a cable. Although not required to use Windows 98, Windows supports the use of the **Microsoft IntelliMouse** (Figure 1-3). The IntelliMouse contains three buttons, the primary mouse button, the secondary mouse button, and the wheel button between the primary and secondary mouse buttons. Typically, the **primary mouse button** is the left mouse button and the **secondary mouse button** is the right mouse button although Windows 98 allows you to switch them. In this book, the left mouse button is the primary mouse button and the right mouse button is the secondary mouse button. The function the **wheel button** and wheel perform depends on the software application being used. If the mouse connected to your computer is not an IntelliMouse, it will not have a wheel button between the primary and secondary mouse buttons. Using the mouse, you can perform the following operations: (1) point; (2) click; (3) right-click; (4) double-click; (5) drag; and (6) right-drag. These operations are demonstrated on the following pages.

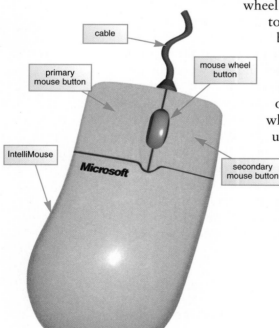

cable

primary mouse button

mouse wheel button

IntelliMouse

Microsoft

secondary mouse button

FIGURE 1-3

Point and Click

Point means you move the mouse across a flat surface until the mouse pointer rests on the item of choice on the desktop. As you move the mouse across a flat surface, the movement of a ball on the underside of the mouse (Figure 1-4) is sensed electronically, and the mouse pointer moves across the desktop in the same direction.

Click means you press and release the primary mouse button, which in this book is the left mouse button. In most cases, you must point to an item before you click. To become acquainted with the use of the mouse, perform the following steps to point to and click various objects on the desktop.

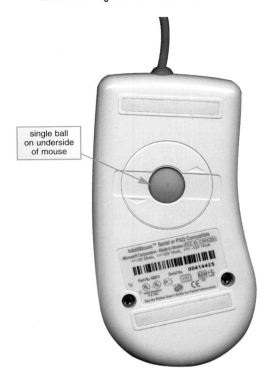

single ball on underside of mouse

FIGURE 1-4

 To Point and Click

1 **Point to the Start button on the taskbar by moving the mouse across a flat surface until the mouse pointer rests on the Start button.**

The mouse pointer on the Start button displays a **ToolTip** *(Click here to begin.) (Figure 1-5). The ToolTip, which provides instructions, displays on the desktop for approximately five seconds. Other ToolTips display on the screen until you move the mouse pointer off the object.*

Start button

ToolTip

mouse pointer

FIGURE 1-5

2 Click the Start button on the taskbar by pressing and releasing the left mouse button.

The Start menu displays and the Start button is recessed on the taskbar (Figure 1-6). A menu is a list of related commands. A command directs Windows 98 to perform a specific action such as shutting down the operating system. Each command on the Start menu consists of an icon and a command name. A right arrow follows some commands to indicate pointing to the command will open a submenu. Three commands (Run, Log Off Steven Forsythe, and Shut Down) are followed by an ellipsis (...) to indicate more information is required to execute these commands.

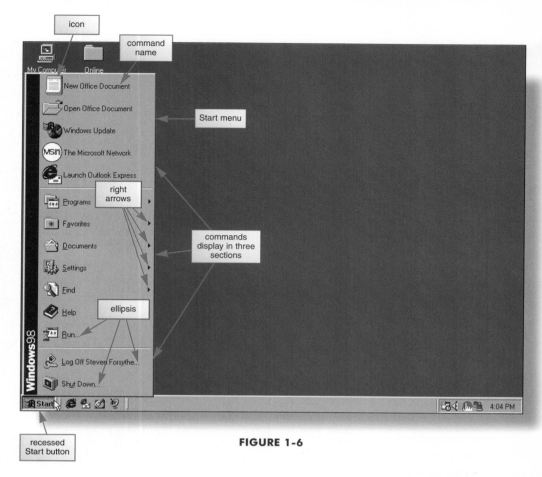

FIGURE 1-6

3 Point to Programs on the Start menu.

When you point to Programs, Windows 98 highlights the Programs command on the Start menu and the Programs submenu displays (Figure 1-7). A submenu, or cascading menu, is a menu that displays when you point to a command that is followed by a right arrow. Whenever you point to a command on a menu, the command is highlighted.

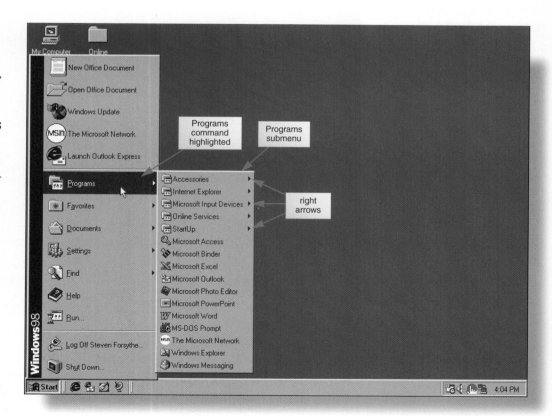

FIGURE 1-7

4 **Point to an open area of the desktop and then click the open area of the desktop.**

The Start menu and Programs submenu close (Figure 1-8). The mouse pointer points to the desktop. To close a menu anytime, click any open area of the desktop except on the menu itself. The Start button is no longer recessed.

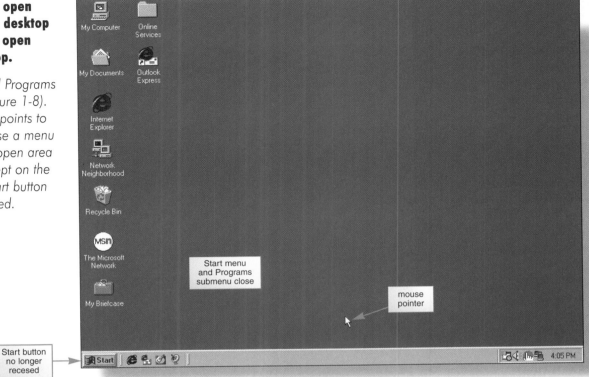

FIGURE 1-8

The Start menu in Figure 1-6 is divided into three sections. The top section contains commands to create or open a Microsoft Office document (New Office Document and Open Office Document), launch the Windows Update application (Windows Update), connect to The Microsoft Network (The Microsoft Network), and launch the Outlook Express application (Launch Outlook Express); the middle section contains commands to launch an application, work with documents or Web sites, customize options, and search for files or Help (Programs, Favorites, Documents, Settings, Find, Help, and Run); and the bottom section contains basic operating tasks (Log Off Steven Forsythe and Shut Down).

When you click an object such as the Start button in Figure 1-6, you must point to the object before you click. In the steps that follow, the instruction that directs you to point to a particular item and then click is, Click the particular item. For example, Click the Start button means point to the Start button and then click.

Right-Click

Right-click means you press and release the secondary mouse button, which in this book is the right mouse button. As directed when using the primary mouse button for clicking an object, normally you will point to an object before you right-click it. Perform the steps on the next page to right-click the desktop.

More About

Buttons

Buttons on the desktop and in programs are an integral part of Windows 98. When you point to them, their function displays in a ToolTip. When you click them, they appear to indent on the screen to mimic what would happen if you pushed an actual button. All buttons in Windows 98 behave in the same manner.

More About

The Right Mouse Button

Earlier versions of Microsoft Windows made little use of the right mouse button. In Windows 98, you will find using the right mouse button essential.

To Right-Click

1 **Point to an open area of the desktop and then press and release the right mouse button.**

*A shortcut menu displays (Figure 1-9). The shortcut menu consists of nine commands. Right-clicking an object, such as the desktop, opens a **shortcut menu** that contains a set of commands specifically for use with that object. When a command on a menu appears dimmed, such as the Paste Shortcut command, that command is unavailable.*

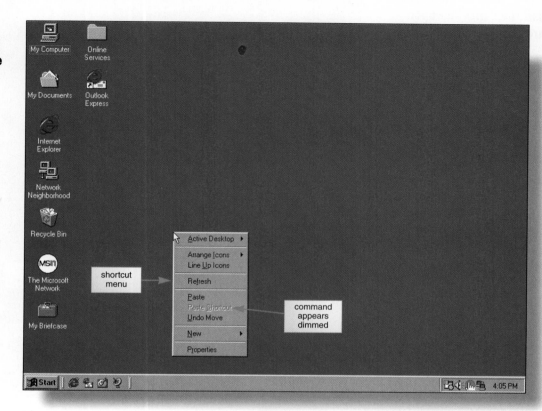

shortcut menu

command appears dimmed

FIGURE 1-9

2 **Point to New on the shortcut menu.**

When you move the mouse pointer to the New command, Windows 98 highlights the New command and opens the New submenu (Figure 1-10). The New submenu contains a variety of commands. The number of commands and the actual commands that display on your computer may be different.

3 **Point to an open area of the desktop and click the open area to remove the shortcut menu and the New submenu.**

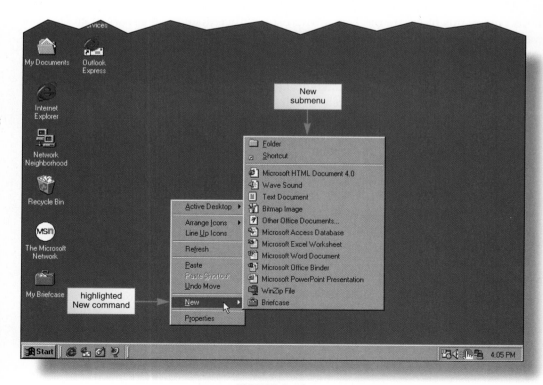

New submenu

highlighted New command

FIGURE 1-10

Whenever you right-click an object, a shortcut menu (also referred to as an object menu) will display. As you will see, the use of shortcut menus speeds up your work and adds flexibility to your interface with the computer.

Double-Click

Double-click means you quickly press and release the left mouse button twice without moving the mouse. In most cases, you must point to an item before you double-click. Perform the following step to open the My Computer window on the desktop by double-clicking the My Computer icon.

Steps To Open a Window by Double-Clicking

1 Point to the My Computer icon on the desktop and then double-click by quickly pressing and releasing the left mouse button twice without moving the mouse.

The My Computer window opens (Figure 1-11). The recessed My Computer button is added to the taskbar button area.

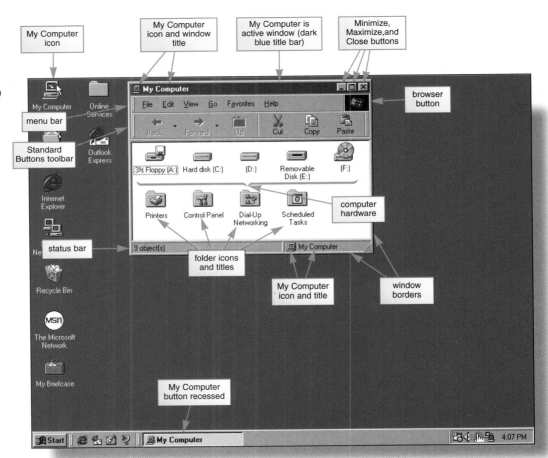

FIGURE 1-11

The My Computer window, the only open window, is the active window. The **active window** is the window currently being used. Whenever you click an object that can be opened, such as the My Computer icon, Windows 98 will open the object; and the open object will be identified by a recessed button in the taskbar button area. The recessed button identifies the active window.

The contents of the My Computer window on your computer may be different from the contents of the My Computer window in Figure 1-11.

My Computer

The trade press and media have poked fun at the icon name, My Computer. One wag said no one should use Windows 98 for more than five minutes without changing the name (which is easily done). Microsoft responds that in their usability labs, beginning computer users found the name, My Computer, easier to understand.

The My Computer Window

Because Windows 98 is easily customized, the My Computer window on your computer may not resemble the window in Figure 1-11 on the previous page. If this is the case, check the commands on the View menu by clicking View on the menu bar. If a check mark precedes the as Web Page command, click the as Web Page command. If a large dot does not precede the Large Icons command, click the Large Icons command.

Minimizing Windows

Windows management on the Windows 98 desktop is important in order to keep the desktop uncluttered. You will find yourself frequently minimizing windows and then later reopening them with a click of a button in the taskbar button area.

My Computer Window

The thin line, or **window border**, surrounding the My Computer window in Figure 1-11 on the previous page determines its shape and size. The **title bar** at the top of the window contains a small icon that is the same as the icon on the desktop and the **window title** (My Computer) that identifies the window. The color of the title bar (dark blue) and the recessed My Computer button in the taskbar button area indicate the My Computer window is the active window. The color of the active window on your computer might be different from the dark blue color shown in Figure 1-11.

Clicking the icon at the left on the title bar will open the **System menu**, which contains commands to carry out the actions associated with the My Computer window. At the right on the title bar are three buttons, the Minimize button, the Maximize button, and the Close button, that can be used to specify the size of the window and close the window.

The **menu bar**, which is the horizontal bar below the title bar of a window (see Figure 1-11 on the previous page), contains a list of menu names for the My Computer window: File, Edit, View, Go, Favorites, and Help. One letter in each menu name is underlined. You can open a menu by clicking the menu name on the menu bar or by typing the corresponding underlined letter on the keyboard in combination with the ALT key. At the right end of the menu bar is a button containing the Windows logo. Clicking this button starts the Microsoft Internet Explorer Web browser and displays one of the Web pages in the Microsoft Web site in the browser window.

Below the menu bar is the **Standard Buttons toolbar** containing buttons that allow you to navigate through open windows on the desktop (Back, Forward, and Up) and copy and move text within a window or between windows (Cut, Copy, and Paste). Additional buttons display when the size of the window is increased. Each button contains a **text label** and an icon describing its function.

The area below the Standard Buttons toolbar contains nine icons. A title below each icon identifies the icon. The five icons in the top row, called **drive icons**, represent a 3½ Floppy (A:) drive, a Hard disk (C:) drive, a different area on the same hard disk (D:), a Removable Disk (E:) drive, and a CD-ROM drive (F:).

The four icons in the second row are folders. A **folder** is an object created to contain related documents, applications, and other folders. A folder in Windows 98 contains items in much the same way a folder on your desk contains items.

A message at the left on the **status bar** located at the bottom of the window indicates the right panel contains nine objects (see Figure 1-11 on the previous page). The My Computer icon and My Computer icon title display to the right of the message on the status bar.

Minimize Button

Two buttons on the title bar of a window, the Minimize button and the Maximize button, allow you to control the way a window displays or does not display on the desktop. When you click the **Minimize button** (see Figure 1-11 on the previous page), the My Computer window no longer displays on the desktop and the recessed My Computer button in the taskbar button area changes to a non-recessed button. A minimized window is still open but it does not display on the screen. To minimize and then redisplay the My Computer window, complete these steps.

To Minimize and Redisplay a Window

1 Point to the Minimize button on the title bar of the My Computer window.

The mouse pointer points to the Minimize button on the My Computer window title bar (Figure 1-12). A ToolTip displays below the Minimize button and the My Computer button in the taskbar button area is recessed.

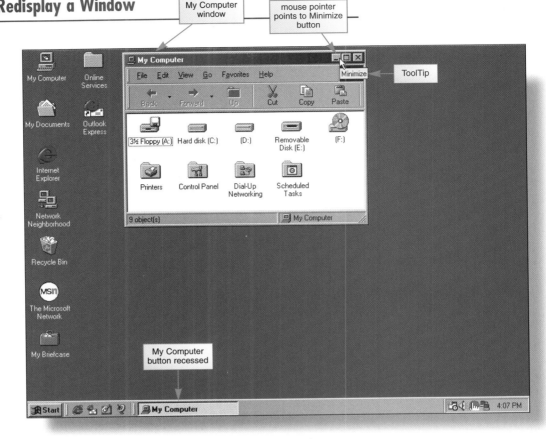

FIGURE 1-12

2 Click the Minimize button.

When you minimize the My Compuer window, Windows 98 removes the My Computer window from the desktop and the My Computer button changes to a non-recessed button (Figure 1-13).

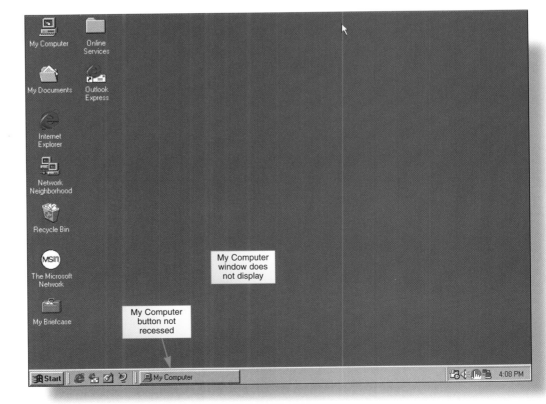

FIGURE 1-13

3 **Click the My Computer button in the taskbar button area.**

The My Computer window displays on the desktop in the same place and size as it was before being minimized (Figure 1-14). In addition, the My Computer window is the active window because it contains the dark blue title bar, and the My Computer button in the taskbar button area is recessed.

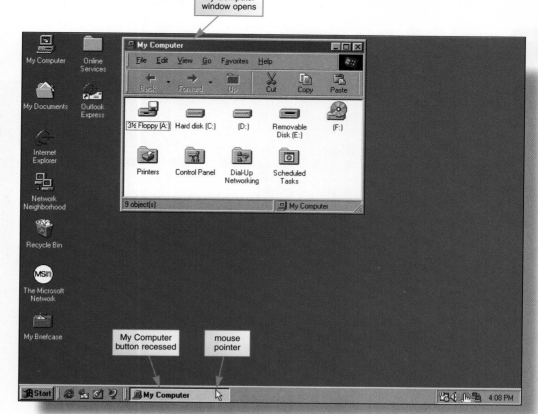

FIGURE 1-14

Whenever a window is minimized, it does not display on the desktop but a non-recessed button for the window does display in the taskbar button area. Whenever you want a minimized window to display and be the active window, click its button in the taskbar button area.

Maximize and Restore Buttons

Sometimes when information is displayed in a window, the information is not completely visible. One method to display the entire contents of a window is to enlarge the window using the **Maximize button**. The Maximize button maximizes a window so the window fills the entire screen, making it easier to see the contents of the window. When a window is maximized, the **Restore button** replaces the Maximize button on the title bar. Clicking the Restore button will return the window to its size before maximizing. To maximize and restore the My Computer window, complete the following steps.

Maximizing Windows

Many application programs run in a maximized window by default. Often you will find that you want to work with maximized windows.

Steps To Maximize and Restore a Window

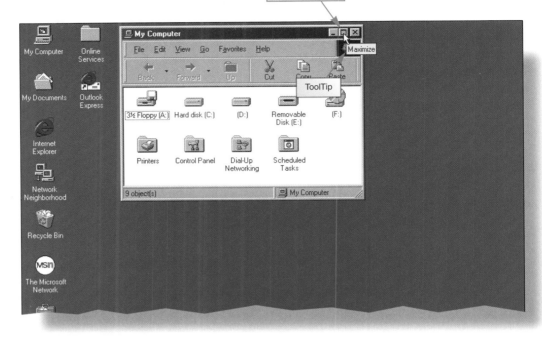

1 **Point to the Maximize button on the title bar of the My Computer window (Figure 1-15).**

FIGURE 1-15

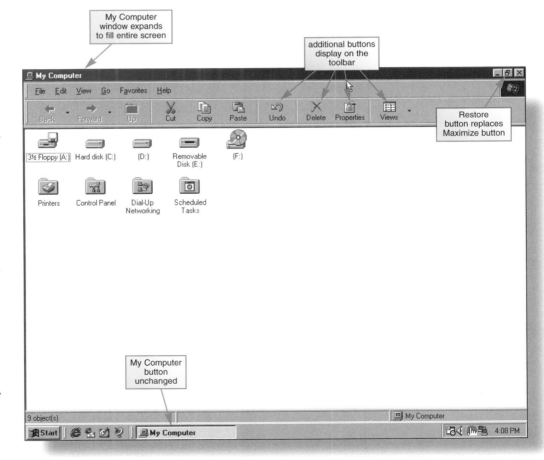

2 **Click the Maximize button.**

*The My Computer window expands so it and the taskbar fill the entire screen (Figure 1-16). The Restore button replaces the Maximize button and the My Computer button in the taskbar button area does not change. The My Computer window is still the active window and additional buttons display on the Standard Buttons toolbar that allow you to undo a previous action (**Undo**), delete text (**Delete**), display the properties of an object (**Properties**), and change the desktop view (**Views**).*

FIGURE 1-16

3 Point to the Restore button on the title bar of the My Computer window (Figure 1-17).

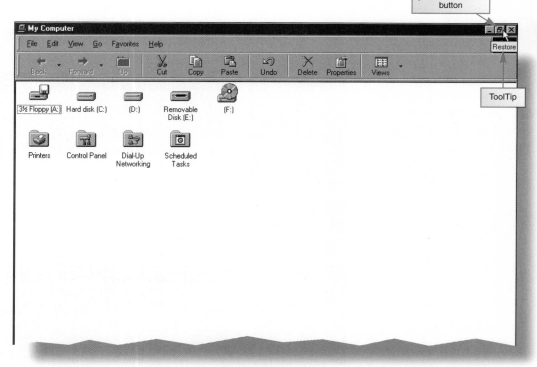

FIGURE 1-17

4 Click the Restore button.

The My Computer window returns to the size and position it occupied before being maximized (Figure 1-18). The My Computer button does not change. The Maximize button replaces the Restore button.

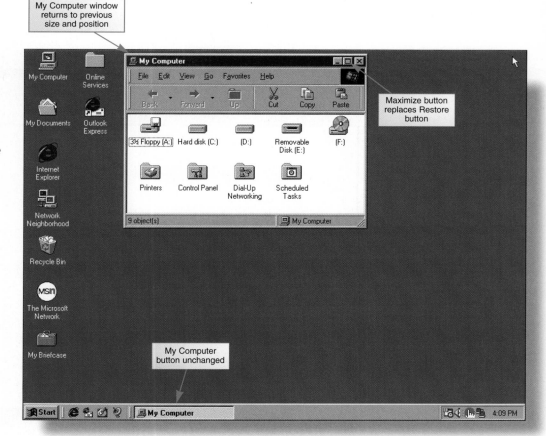

FIGURE 1-18

When a window is maximized, such as in Figure 1-16 on page WIN 1.17, you also can minimize the window by clicking the Minimize button. If, after minimizing the window, you click its button in the taskbar button area, the window will return to its maximized size.

Close Button

The **Close button** on the title bar of a window closes the window and removes the window button from the taskbar. To close and then reopen the My Computer window, complete the following steps.

 To Close a Window and Reopen a Window

1 **Point to the Close button on the title bar of the My Computer window (Figure 1-19).**

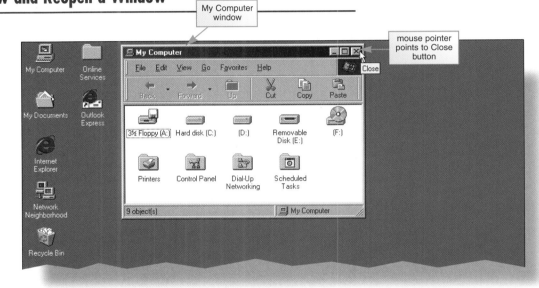

FIGURE 1-19

2 **Click the Close button.**

The My Computer window closes and the My Computer button no longer displays in the taskbar button area (Figure 1-20).

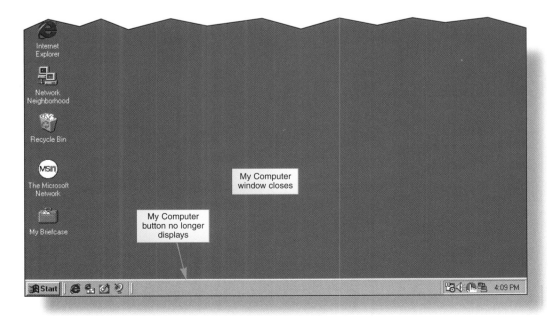

FIGURE 1-20

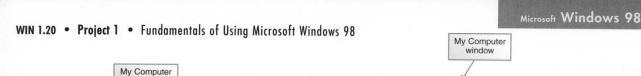
3 **Point to and double-click the My Computer icon on the desktop.**

The My Computer window opens and displays on the screen (Figure 1-21). The My Computer button displays in the taskbar button area.

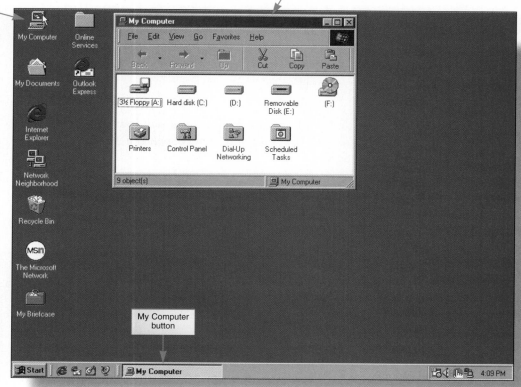

FIGURE 1-21

Drag

Drag means you point to an item, hold down the left mouse button, move the item to the desired location, and then release the left mouse button. You can move any open window to another location on the desktop by pointing to the title bar of the window and dragging the window. To drag the My Computer window to another location on the desktop, perform the following steps.

 **To Move an Object by Dragging**

1 **Point to the My Computer window title bar (Figure 1-22).**

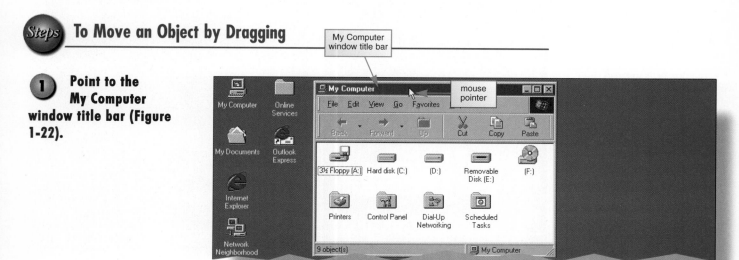

FIGURE 1-22

2 Hold down the left mouse button, move the mouse so the window moves to the center of the desktop, and release the left mouse button.

As you drag the mouse, the My Computer window moves across the desktop. When you release the left mouse button, the window displays in its new location (Figure 1-23).

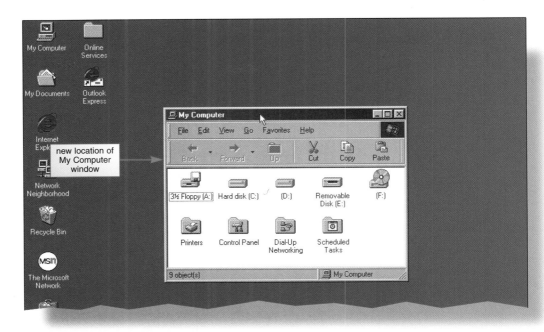

FIGURE 1-23

Sizing a Window by Dragging

You can use dragging for more than just moving an object. For example, you can drag the border of a window to change the size of the window. To change the size of the My Computer window, perform the following step.

 To Size a Window by Dragging

1 Position the mouse pointer over the lower-right corner of the My Computer window until the mouse pointer changes to a two-headed arrow. Drag the lower-right corner upward and to the right until the window on your desktop resembles the window shown in Figure 1-24.

As you drag the lower-right corner, the window changes size and a vertical scroll bar displays (Figure 1-24). Five of the nine icons in the window are visible in the resized window in Figure 1-24.

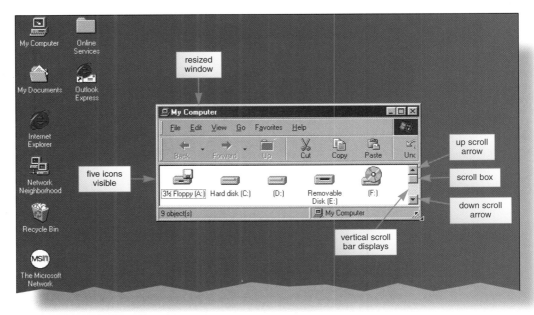

FIGURE 1-24

More About

Window Sizing

Windows 98 remembers the size of the window when you close the window. When you reopen the window, it will display in the same size as when you closed it.

More About

Scrolling

Most people will either maximize a window or size it so all the objects in the window are visible to avoid scrolling because scrolling takes time. It is more efficient not to have to scroll in a window.

A scroll bar is a bar that displays at the right edge and/or bottom edge of a window when the window contents are not completely visible. A vertical scroll bar contains an **up scroll arrow**, a **down scroll arrow**, and a **scroll box** that enable you to view areas of the window not currently visible. A vertical scroll bar displays in the My Computer window shown in Figure 1-24 on the previous page.

The size of the scroll box in any window is dependent on the amount of the window that is not visible. The smaller the scroll box, the more of the window that is not visible. In Figure 1-24, the scroll box occupies approximately half of the scroll bar. This indicates that approximately half of the contents of the window are not visible. If the scroll box were a tiny rectangle, a large portion of the window would not be visible.

In addition to dragging a corner of a window, you also can drag any of the borders of a window. If you drag a vertical border, such as the right border, you can move the border left or right. If you drag a horizontal border, such as the bottom border, you can move the border of the window up or down.

As mentioned earlier, maximizing a window is one method to enlarge a window and display more information in the window. Dragging a window to enlarge the window is a second method to display information in a window that is not visible.

Scrolling in a Window

Previously, two methods were shown to display information that was not completely visible in the My Computer window. These methods were maximizing the My Computer window and changing the size of the My Computer window. A third method uses the scroll bar in the window.

Scrolling can be accomplished in three ways: (1) click the scroll arrows; (2) click the scroll bar; and (3) drag the scroll box. On the following pages, you will use the scroll bar to scroll the contents of the My Computer window. Perform the following steps to scroll the My Computer window using the scroll arrows.

To Scroll a Window Using Scroll Arrows

1 **Point to the down scroll arrow on the vertical scroll bar (Figure 1-25).**

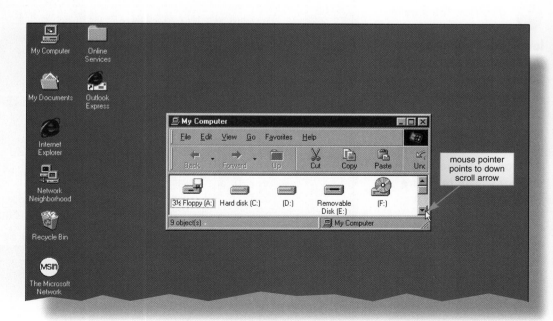

FIGURE 1-25

2 **Click the down scroll arrow one time.**

The window scrolls down (the icons move up in the window) and displays the tops of the icons previously not visible (Figure 1-26). Because the window size does not change when you scroll, the contents of the window will change, as seen in the difference between Figure 1-25 and Figure 1-26.

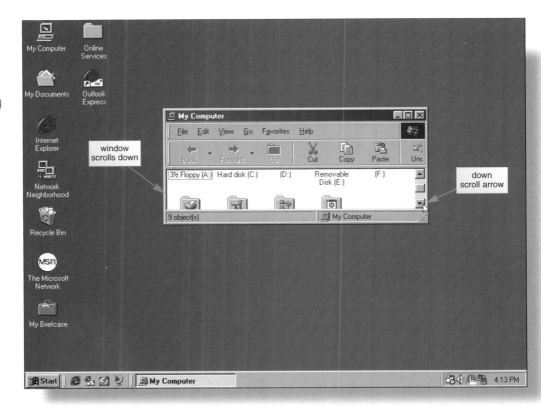

FIGURE 1-26

3 **Click the down scroll arrow two more times.**

The scroll box moves to the bottom of the scroll bar and the remaining icons in the window display (Figure 1-27).

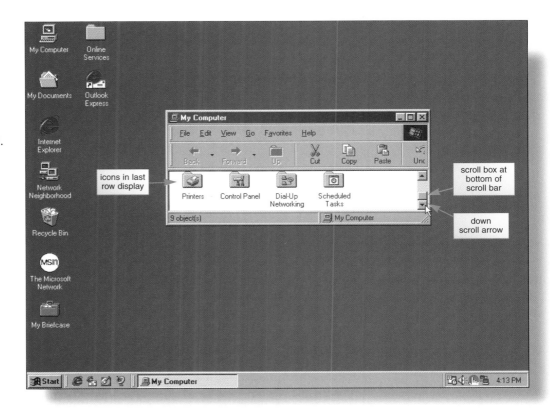

FIGURE 1-27

More About

The Scroll Bar

In many application programs, clicking the scroll bar will move the window a full screen's worth of information up or down. You can step through a word processing document screen by screen, for example, by clicking the scroll bar.

You can scroll continuously through a window using scroll arrows by pointing to the up or down scroll arrow and holding down the left mouse button. The window continues to scroll until you release the left mouse button or you reach the top or bottom of the window. You can also scroll by clicking the scroll bar itself. When you click the scroll bar, the window moves up or down a greater distance than when you click the scroll arrows.

The third way in which you can scroll through a window to view its contents is by dragging the scroll box. When you drag the scroll box, the window moves up or down as you drag.

Being able to view the contents of a window by scrolling is an important Windows 98 skill because in many cases the entire contents of a window are not visible.

More About

The Scroll Box

Dragging the scroll box is the most efficient technique to scroll long distances. In many application programs, such as Microsoft Word, as you scroll using the scroll box, the page number of the document displays next to the scroll box.

Resizing a Window

After moving and resizing a window, you may wish to return the window to approximately its original size. To return the My Computer window to about its original size, complete the following steps.

TO RESIZE A WINDOW

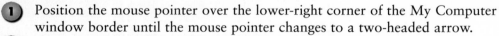

1 Position the mouse pointer over the lower-right corner of the My Computer window border until the mouse pointer changes to a two-headed arrow.

2 Drag the lower-right corner of the My Computer window until the window is the same size as shown in Figure 1-23 on page WIN 1.21, and then release the mouse button.

The My Computer window is approximately the same size as before you made it smaller.

More About

Scrolling Guidelines

General scrolling guidelines: (1) To scroll short distances (line by line), click the scroll arrows; (2) To scroll one screen at a time, click the scroll bar; and (3) To scroll long distances, drag the scroll box.

Closing a Window

After you have completed your work in a window, normally you will close the window. To close the My Computer window, complete the following steps.

TO CLOSE A WINDOW

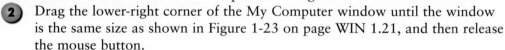

1 Point to the Close button on the right of the title bar in the My Computer window.

2 Click the Close button.

The My Computer window closes and the desktop contains no open windows.

More About

Right-Dragging

Right-dragging was not available on some earlier versions of Windows, so you might find people familiar with Windows not even considering right-dragging. Because it always produces a shortcut menu, however, right-dragging is the safest way to drag.

Right-Drag

Right-drag means you point to an item, hold down the right mouse button, move the item to the desired location, and then release the right mouse button. When you right-drag an object, a shortcut menu displays. The shortcut menu contains commands specifically for use with the object being dragged. To right-drag the My Briefcase icon to the right of its current position on the desktop, perform the following steps. If the My Briefcase icon does not display on your desktop, you will be unable to perform Step 1 through Step 3 that follow.

To Right-Drag

1 **Point to the My Briefcase icon on** the desktop, hold down the right mouse button, drag the icon to the right toward the middle of the desktop, and then release the right mouse button.

The dimmed My Briefcase icon and a shortcut menu display in the middle of the desktop (Figure 1-28). The My Briefcase icon remains at its original location. The shortcut menu contains four commands: Move Here, Copy Here, Create Shortcut(s) Here, and Cancel. The Move Here command in bold (dark) type identifies what would happen if you were to drag the My Briefcase icon with the left mouse button.

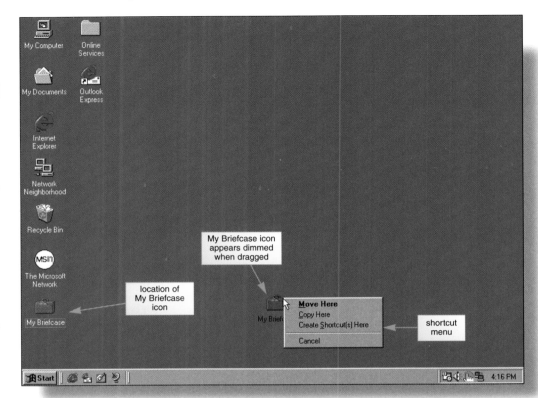

FIGURE 1-28

2 **Point to Cancel on the shortcut menu.**

The Cancel command is highlighted (Figure 1-29).

3 **Click Cancel on the shortcut menu.**

The shortcut menu and the dragged My Briefcase icon disappear from the screen.

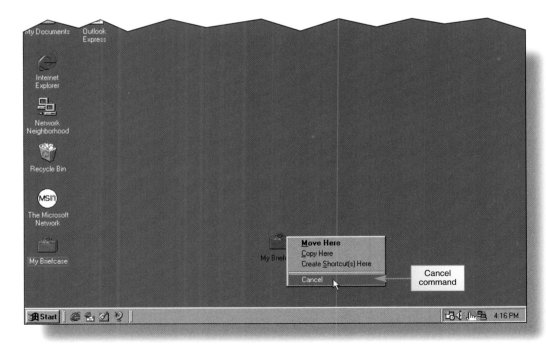

FIGURE 1-29

Whenever you begin an operation but do not want to complete the operation, you can click Cancel on a shortcut menu or click the Cancel button in a dialog box. The **Cancel** command will reset anything you have done in the operation.

If you click **Move Here** on the shortcut menu shown in Figure 1-28 on the previous page, Windows 98 will move the icon from its current location to the new location. If you click **Copy Here**, the icon will be copied to the new location and two icons will display on the desktop. Windows 98 automatically will give the second icon a different title. If you click **Create Shortcut(s) Here**, a special object called a shortcut will be created.

Although you can move icons by dragging with the primary (left) mouse button and by right-dragging with the secondary (right) mouse button, it is strongly suggested you right-drag because a menu displays and you can specify the exact operation you want to occur. When you drag using the left mouse button, a default operation takes place and the operation may not do what you want.

Summary of Mouse and Windows Operations

You have seen how to use the mouse to point, click, right-click, double-click, drag, and right-drag in order to accomplish certain tasks on the desktop. The use of a mouse is an important skill when using Windows 98. In addition, you have learned how to move around and use windows on the Windows 98 desktop.

The Keyboard and Keyboard Shortcuts

The **keyboard** is an input device on which you manually key, or type, data. Figure 1-30a shows the enhanced IBM 101-key keyboard, and Figure 1-30b shows a Microsoft Natural keyboard designed specifically for use with Windows. Many tasks you accomplish with a mouse also can be accomplished using a keyboard.

To perform tasks using the keyboard, you must understand the notation used to identify which keys to press. This notation is used throughout Windows 98 to identify **keyboard shortcuts**.

FIGURE 1-30a

FIGURE 1-30b

Keyboard shortcuts consist of: (1) pressing a single key (example: press the ENTER key); or (2) pressing and holding down one key and pressing a second key, as shown by two key names separated by a plus sign (example: press CTRL+ESC). For example, to obtain Help about Windows 98, you can press the F1 key; to open the Start menu, hold down the CTRL key and then press the ESC key (press CTRL+ESC).

Often, computer users will use keyboard shortcuts for operations they perform frequently. For example, many users find pressing the F1 key to launch Windows 98 Help easier than using the Start menu as shown later in this project. As a user, you probably will find the combination of keyboard and mouse operations that particularly suit you, but it is strongly recommended that generally you use the mouse.

More *About*

The Microsoft Keyboard

The Microsoft keyboard in Figure 1-30(b) not only has special keys for Windows 98, but also is designed ergonomically so you type with your hands apart. It takes a little time to get used to, but several authors on the Shelly Cashman Series writing team report they type faster with more accuracy and less fatigue when using the keyboard.

The Windows 98 Desktop Views

Windows 98 provides several ways to view your desktop and the windows that open on the desktop. The three desktop views include the Web style, Classic style, and Custom style. The desktop view you choose will affect the appearance of your desktop, how you open and work with windows on the desktop, and how you work with the files and folders on your computer.

The Classic Style

The **Classic style** causes the desktop and the objects on the desktop to display and function as they did in Windows 95, a previous version of Windows. When you choose the Classic style as your desktop view, the desktop is referred to as the **Classic Windows Desktop**. The Classic Windows Desktop is similar to the desktop shown in Figure 1-2 on page WIN 1.6 and is shown again in Figure 1-31.

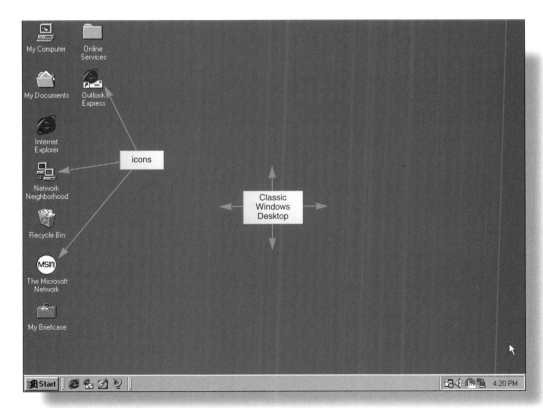

FIGURE 1-31

The icons on the desktop shown in Figure 1-31 on the previous page behave as they did in Windows 95. You double-click an icon to open its window and display its button in the taskbar button area. For example, double-clicking the My Computer icon on the desktop opens the My Computer window and displays the My Computer button in the taskbar button area (Figure 1-32).

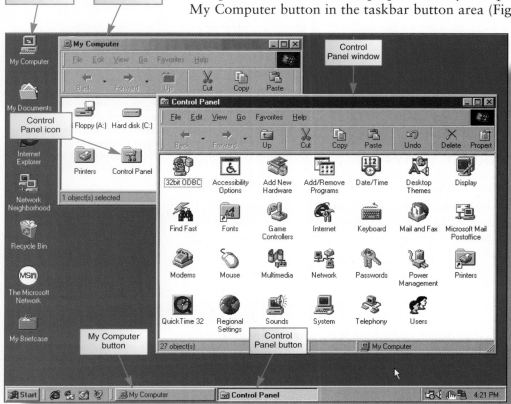

FIGURE 1-32

If, after opening the My Computer window, you want to display the contents of a folder in the My Computer window, you double-click the folder icon to open its window and display its taskbar button. For example, you might double-click the Control Panel folder icon in the My Computer window to open its window and display its taskbar button (Figure 1-32).

Double-clicking the Control Panel folder icon opens a second window on the desktop (Control Panel window) and places a second button (Control Panel button) in the taskbar button area.

The Internet and World Wide Web

The second desktop view available in Windows 98 is the Web style. The Web style uses the Internet and an area of the Internet called the World Wide Web to retrieve and display information on the desktop.

The **Internet** is a worldwide group of connected computer networks that allows public access to information on thousands of subjects and gives users the ability to send messages and obtain products and services. Computers connected to the Internet deliver information using a variety of computer media, including text, graphics, sound, video clips, and animation. On the Internet, this multimedia capability is called **hypermedia**, which is any variety of computer media. Underlined text, a picture, or an icon used to access hypermedia is called a **hyperlink**, or simply a **link**. Clicking a hyperlink on a computer in Los Angeles could cause a picture stored on a computer in Germany to display on the desktop of the computer in Los Angeles.

The collection of hyperlinks throughout the Internet creates an interconnected network of links called the **World Wide Web**, also referred to as the **Web**. Each computer within the Web that can be referenced by a hyperlink is called a **Web site**. Hundreds of thousands of Web sites around the world can be accessed through the Internet. Graphics, text, and other hypermedia are stored in files called **hypertext documents**, or **Web pages**. Figure 1-33 illustrates one of several Web pages in the Web site operated by ESPN, a popular sports broadcasting company.

FIGURE 1-33

The Web page shown in Figure 1-33 contains a variety of multimedia (text, graphics, and animation) and hyperlinks. A unique address, called a **Uniform Resource Locator (URL)**, identifies each Web page in a Web site. The URL for the ESPN Web page shown in Figure 1-33, http://espn.sportszone.com, displays in the Address bar at the top of the http://espn.sportszone.com/ – Microsoft Internet Explorer window.

A software tool, called a **Web browser**, allows you to locate a Web page if you know the URL for the Web page. The **Microsoft Internet Explorer 4 Web browser** included with Windows 98 displays the Web page shown in Figure 1-33. Clicking a hyperlink on the Web page causes the browser to locate the associated Web page and display its contents in the same window.

The Web Style

In **Web style**, the icon titles on the desktop are underlined similarly to the hyperlinks in a Web page, and the desktop is referred to as the **Active Desktop™** (Figure 1-34).

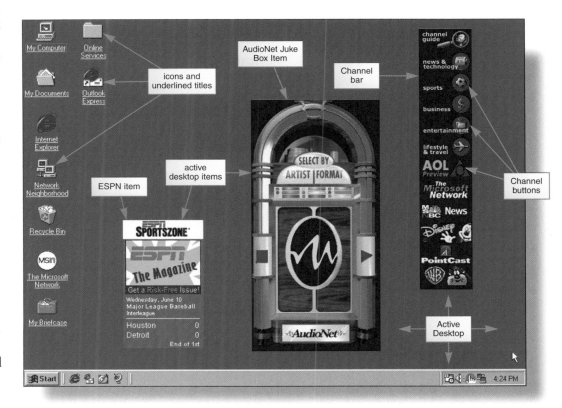

FIGURE 1-34

The Web style causes the Channel bar to display on the desktop and allows you to place other objects, called **active desktop items**, on the desktop (see Figure 1-34 on the previous page). The **Channel bar** contains twelve **Channel buttons** (channel guide, news & technology, sports, business, entertainment, lifestyle & travel, AOL Preview, The Microsoft Network, MSNBC News, Disney, PointCast, and WB) that assist you in placing desktop items on the Active Desktop.

Two active desktop items (ESPN SportsZone™ and AudioNet Juke Box) display on the desktop shown in Figure 1-34. The **ESPN SportsZone™ item** displays the latest sports scores from the ESPN SportsZone™ Web site shown in Figure 1-33 on the previous page and updates the scores periodically. The **AudioNet Juke Box item** allows you to select and listen to hundreds of audio CDs from the AudioNet Web site on the Internet.

Unlike the Classic style, the icon titles on the desktop are underlined and you click an icon to open its window and display its taskbar button. When you click an icon on the desktop, such as the My Computer folder icon, the My Computer window opens on the desktop with a different look and feel than the My Computer window that opens when you double-click its icon in Classic style (Figure 1-35). In Windows terminology, this look and feel is referred to as **displaying a folder as a Web page**.

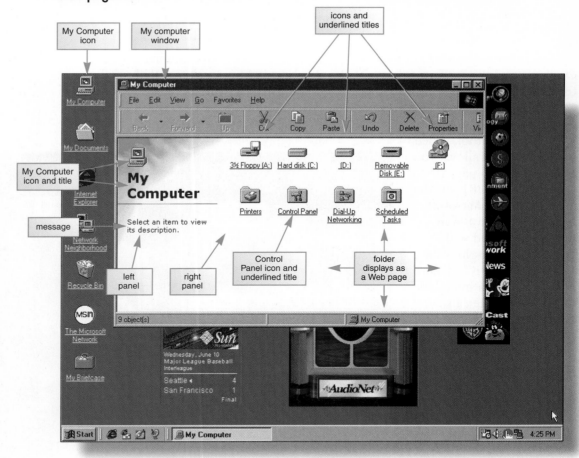

FIGURE 1-35

The My Computer window displays as a Web page with the area below the Standard Buttons toolbar divided into two panels. The My Computer icon and its icon title, My Computer, display at the top of the left panel. The text, Select an item to view its description, displays below the icon and title in the left panel. The right panel of the My Computer window contains nine icons and their underlined titles.

In Classic style, double-clicking the Control Panel icon in the My Computer window opened a second window on the desktop and displayed a second taskbar button (see Figure 1-32 on page WIN 1.28). In Web style, you click instead of double-click a folder icon in the My Computer window to display the contents of the drive or folder. To display the contents of the Control Panel folder, you click the Control Panel icon in the My Computer window (Figure 1-36).

The Control Panel window opens in the same window in which the My Computer window was displayed, and the Control Panel button replaces the My Computer button in the taskbar button area. The Control Panel displays as a Web page with the left panel containing information about the Control Panel and the right panel containing the icons in the Control Panel folder.

If, after displaying the Control Panel window, you again want to display the My Computer window, you can click the Back button on the Standard Buttons toolbar to replace the Control Panel window and taskbar button with the My Computer window and taskbar button.

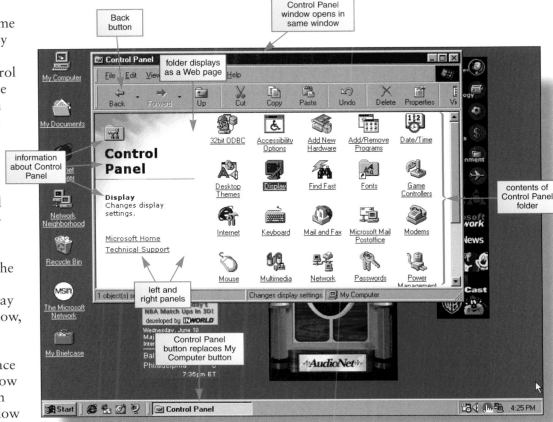

FIGURE 1-36

The Custom Style

The third desktop view available in Windows 98 is the Custom style. The **Custom style** allows you to pick and choose the options you prefer, including a combination of Classic style and Web style settings. The options include being able to: (1) view the Active Desktop™ or the Classic Windows Desktop; (2) open a folder in the same window or its own window; (3) view all folders or only folders you select as Web pages; and (4) single-click or double-click an icon.

When Windows 98 is installed on a computer, the desktop view that displays when you launch Windows 98 is the Custom style. The settings that were chosen by Microsoft, referred to as **default settings**, include: (1) viewing the Classic Windows Desktop; (2) opening a folder in the same window; (3) viewing only folders you select as Web pages; and (4) double-clicking to open an item. As a result, you view the Classic Windows Desktop on the desktop, folders open in the same window on the desktop, left and right panels do not display in a window, and you double-click an icon to open its window.

The steps and screens you see in this book assume the default settings of the Custom style, as chosen by Microsoft Corporation, are installed on your computer. If you find this not to be the case, refer to the Preface of this book for instructions to switch the desktop view to the default desktop view or contact your instructor to change the desktop view.

More About

Desktop Views

The Classic style was included in the Windows 98 operating system to allow Windows 95 users to upgrade easily to the newer Windows 98 operating system. Responses from people in the Beta Test program, which is a program designed to test software prior to the public sale of the software, indicated that most Windows 95 users had little difficulty switching to Windows 98, and experienced users liked the Web style and Active Desktop.

Launching an Application Program

One of the basic tasks you can perform using Windows 98 is to launch an application program. A **program** is a set of computer instructions that carries out a task on your computer. An **application program** is a program that allows you to accomplish a specific task for which that program is designed. For example, a **word processing program** is an application program that allows you to create written documents; a **presentation graphics program** is an application program that allows you to create graphic presentations for display on a computer; and a **Web browser program** is an application program that allows you to search for and display Web pages.

The most common activity on a computer is to launch an application program to accomplish tasks using the computer. You can launch an application program in a variety of ways. When several methods are available to accomplish a task, a computer user has the opportunity to try various methods and select the method that best fits his or her needs.

To illustrate the variety of methods available to launch an application program, three methods will be shown to launch the Internet Explorer Web browser program. These methods include using the Start button; using the Quick Launch toolbar; and using an icon on the desktop.

Launching an Application Using the Start Button

The first method to launch an application program is to use the Start menu. Perform the following steps to launch Internet Explorer using the Start menu and Internet Explorer command.

 To Launch a Program Using the Start Menu

1 **Click the Start button on the taskbar. Point to Programs on the Start menu. Point to Internet Explorer on the Programs submenu. Point to Internet Explorer on the Internet Explorer submenu.**

*The Start menu, Programs submenu, and Internet Explorer submenu display (Figure 1-37). The Internet Explorer submenu contains the **Internet Explorer command** to launch the Internet Explorer program. You might find more, fewer, or different commands on the submenus on your computer.*

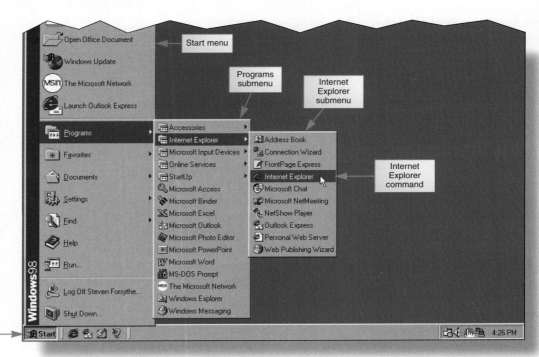

FIGURE 1-37

2 **Click Internet
Explorer.**

*Windows 98 launches the
Internet Explorer program by
opening the MSN.COM,
Welcome Page – Microsoft
Internet Explorer
window on the
desktop, displaying the
Welcome to MSN.COM Web
page in the window, and
adding a recessed button to
the taskbar button area
(Figure 1-38). The URL for
the Web page displays on the
Address bar. Because Web
pages are modified fre-
quently, the Web page that
displays on your desktop may
be different from the Web
page in Figure 1-38.*

3 **Click the Close
button in the
Internet Explorer window.**

*The Microsoft Internet
Explorer window closes.*

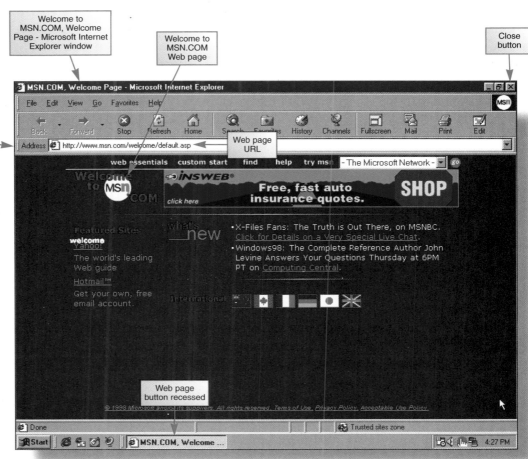

FIGURE 1-38

After you have launched Internet Explorer, you can use the program to search
for and display different Web pages.

Launching an Application Using the Quick Launch Toolbar

The second method to launch an application is to use an icon on the Quick
Launch toolbar. Currently, the Quick Launch toolbar contains four icons that allow
you to launch Internet Explorer, launch Outlook Express, view an uncluttered desktop at any time, and view a list of channels (see Figure 1-39 on the next page). Perform the steps on the next page to launch the Internet Explorer program using the
Launch Internet Explorer Browser icon on the Quick Launch toolbar.

Steps To Launch a Program Using the Quick Launch Toolbar

1 **Point to the Launch Internet Explorer Browser icon on the Quick Launch toolbar (Figure 1-39).**

2 **Click the Launch Internet Explorer Browser icon.**

Windows 98 launches the Internet Explorer program as shown in Figure 1-38 on the previous page.

3 **Click the Close button in the Internet Explorer window.**

Windows 98 closes the Microsoft Internet Explorer window.

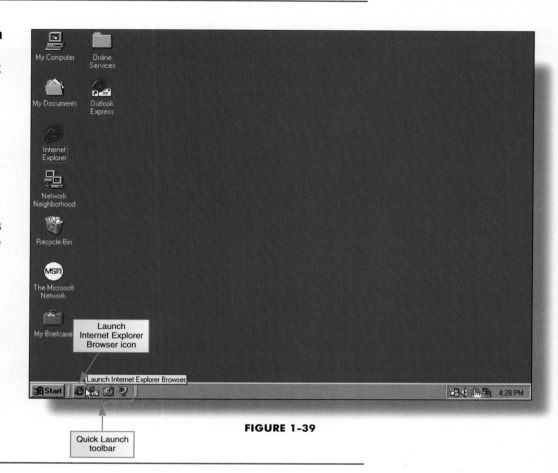

FIGURE 1-39

Launching an Application Using an Icon on the Desktop

The third method to launch an application is to use an icon on the desktop. Perform the following steps to launch the Internet Explorer program using the Internet Explorer icon on the desktop.

To Launch a Program Using an Icon on the Desktop

1 **Point to the Internet Explorer icon on the desktop (Figure 1-40).**

2 **Double-click the Internet Explorer icon.**

Windows 98 launches the Internet Explorer program as shown in Figure 1-38 on page WIN 1.33.

3 **Click the Close button in the Internet Explorer window.**

The Microsoft Internet Explorer window closes.

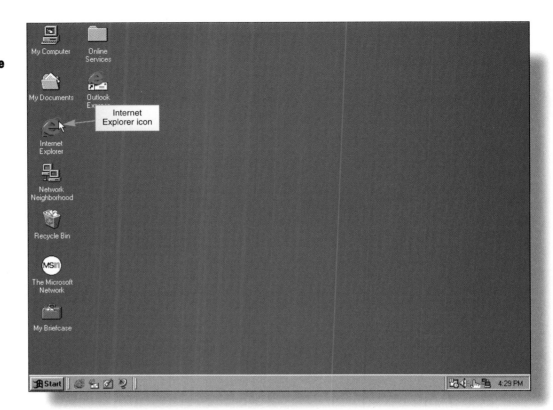

FIGURE 1-40

Windows 98 provides a number of ways in which to accomplish a particular task. Previously, three methods to launch the Internet Explorer program were illustrated. In the remainder of this book, a single set of steps will illustrate how to accomplish a task. Those steps may not be the only way in which the task can be completed. If you can perform the same task using other methods, the Other Ways box specifies the other methods. In each case, the method shown in the steps is the preferred method, but it is important for you to be aware of all the techniques you can use.

Using Windows Help

One of the more powerful application programs for use in Windows 98 is Windows Help. Windows Help is available when using Windows 98, or when using any application program running under Windows 98, to assist you in using Windows 98 and the various application programs. It contains answers to many questions you can ask with respect to Windows 98.

Other **Ways**

1. In open window, click button at right end of menu bar
2. Click Start button, click Run, type iexplore, click OK button

More **About**

Windows 98 Help

If you purchased an operating system or application program five years ago, you received at least one, and more often several, thick and heavy technical manuals that explained the software. With Windows 98, you receive a skinny manual less than 100 pages in length. The online Help feature of Windows 98 replaces reams and reams of printed pages in hard-to-understand technical manuals.

Contents Sheet

Windows Help provides a variety of ways in which to obtain information. One method to find a Help topic involves using the **Contents sheet** to browse through Help topics by category. To illustrate this method, you will use Windows Help to determine how to find a topic in Help. To launch Help, complete the following steps.

 To Launch Windows Help

1 **Click the Start button on the taskbar. Point to Help on the Start menu (Figure 1-41).**

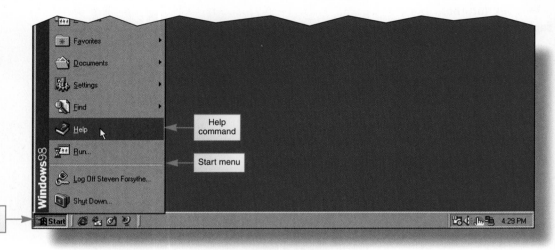

FIGURE 1-41

2 **Click Help. Click the Maximize button on the Windows Help title bar. If the Contents sheet does not display, click the Contents tab.**

*The Windows Help window opens and maximizes (Figure 1-42). The window contains the Help toolbar and two frames. The left frame contains three **tabs** (Contents, Index, and Search). The Contents sheet is visible in the left frame. The right frame contains information about the Welcome to Help topic.*

 Ways

1. Press F1
2. Press WINDOWS+H (WINDOWS key on Microsoft Natural keyboard)

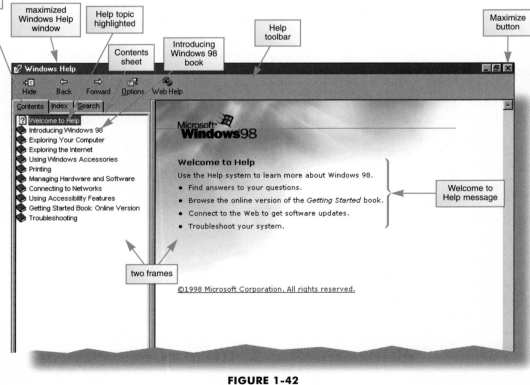

FIGURE 1-42

The Contents sheet contains a **Help topic** preceded by a question mark icon and followed by ten books. Each book consists of a closed book icon followed by a book name. The Help topic, Welcome to Help, is highlighted. In the left frame, a closed book icon indicates that Help topics or more books are contained in the book. The question mark icon indicates a Help topic without any further subdivisions. Clicking either the Index tab or the Search tab in the left frame opens the Index or Search sheet, respectively.

In addition to launching Help by using the Start button, you also can launch Help by pressing the F1 key.

After launching Help, the next step is to find the topic in which you are interested. To find the topic that describes how to find a topic in Help, complete the following steps.

 To Use Help to Find a Topic in Help

1 **Point to the Introducing Windows 98 closed book icon.**

The mouse pointer changes to a hand when positioned on the icon and the Introducing Windows 98 book name displays in blue font and underlined (Figure 1-43).

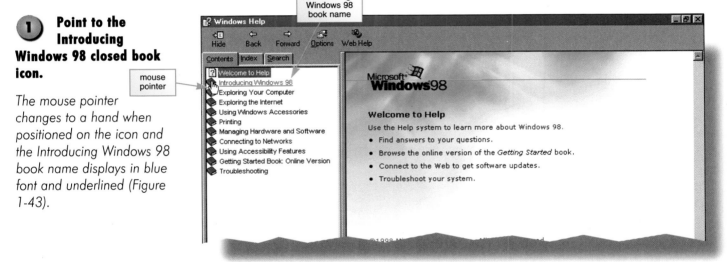

FIGURE 1-43

2 **Click the Introducing Windows 98 closed book icon and then point to the How to Use Help closed book icon.**

Windows 98 opens the Introducing Windows 98 book, changes the closed book icon to an open book icon, highlights the Introducing Windows 98 book name, underlines the How to Use Help book name, and displays the name and underline in blue font (Figure 1-44).

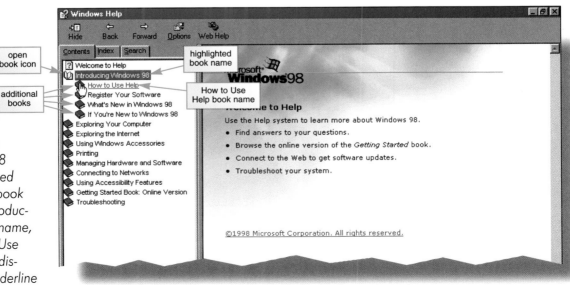

FIGURE 1-44

③ **Click the How to Use Help closed book icon and then point to Find a topic in the opened How to Use Help book.**

Windows 98 opens the How to Use Help book and displays several Help topics in the book, changes the closed book icon to an open book icon, highlights the How to Use Help book name, underlines the Find a topic Help topic name, and displays the topic name and underline in blue font (Figure 1-45).

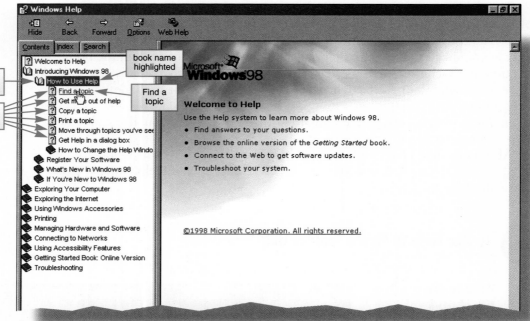

FIGURE 1-45

④ **Click Find a topic. Read the information about finding a Help topic in the right frame of the Windows Help window.**

Windows 98 highlights the Finding a topic Help topic and displays information about finding a Help topic in the right frame of the Windows Help window (Figure 1-46).

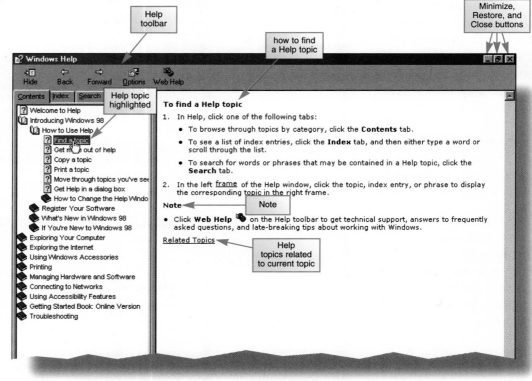

FIGURE 1-46

Other **Ways**

1. Press DOWN ARROW key until book or topic is highlighted, press ENTER, continue until Help topic displays, read Help topic

In Figure 1-46, if you click the **Hide button** on the Help toolbar, Windows 98 hides the tabs in the left frame and displays only the right frame in the Windows Help window. Clicking the **Back button** or **Forward button** displays a previously displayed Help topic in the right frame. Clicking the **Options button** allows you to hide or display the tabs in the left frame, display previously displayed Help topics in the right frame, stop the display of a Help topic, refresh the currently displayed Help topic, access Web Help, and print a Help topic. The **Web Help command** on the Options menu and the **Web Help button** on the Help toolbar allow you to use the Internet to obtain technical support, answers to frequently asked questions, and tips about working with Windows 98. Web Help will be explained in Project 2.

Notice also in Figure 1-46 that the Windows Help title bar contains a Minimize button, Restore button, and Close button. You can minimize or restore the Windows Help window as needed and also close the Windows Help window.

Index Sheet

A second method to find answers to your questions about Windows 98 or application programs running under Windows 98 is the Index sheet. The **Index sheet** lists a large number of index entries, each of which references one or more Help screens. To learn more about the Classic style and Web style, complete the following steps.

 To Use the Help Index Sheet

1 **Click the Index tab. Type** classic style **(the flashing insertion point is positioned in the text box) in the text box. Point to the Display button at the bottom of the left frame.**

The Index sheet displays in the left frame and includes a list of entries that can be referenced (Figure 1-47). When you type an entry, the list automatically scrolls and the entry you type, such as classic style, is highlighted. To see additional entries, use the scroll bar at the right of the list. To highlight an entry in the list, click the entry.

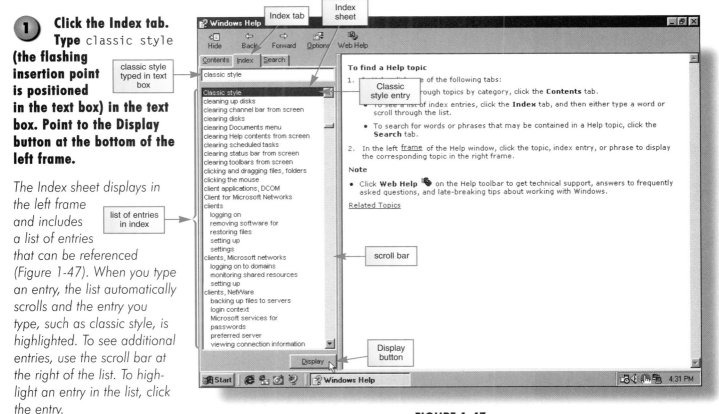

FIGURE 1-47

2 **Click the Display button in the Windows Help window. Point to the Display button in the Topics Found dialog box.**

The Topics Found dialog box displays on top of the Windows Help window and two Help topics display in the dialog box (Figure 1-48). A **dialog box** displays whenever Windows 98 needs to supply information to you or requires you to enter information or select among several options. The first topic, Choosing Web or Classic style for folders, is highlighted. This topic contains information about the Web and Classic styles.

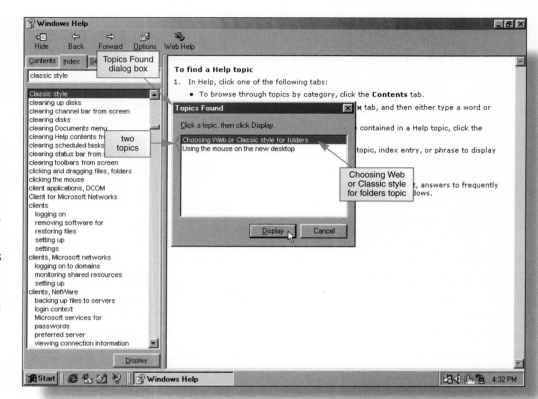

FIGURE 1-48

3 **Click the Display button.**

Information about the Web and Classic style, several hyperlinks, and one related topic displays in the right frame of the Windows Help window (Figure 1-49).

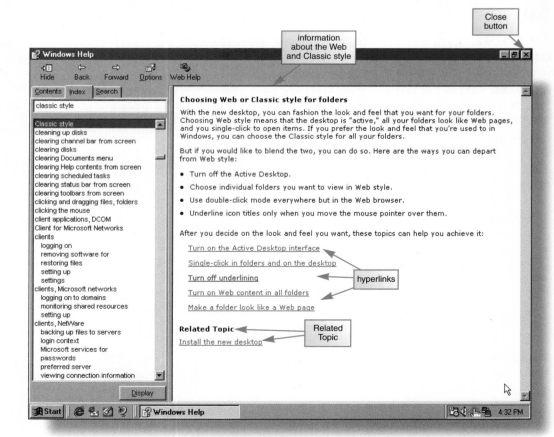

FIGURE 1-49

After viewing the index entries, normally you will close Windows Help. To close Windows Help, complete the following step.

TO CLOSE WINDOWS HELP

1. Click the Close button on the title bar of the Windows Help window.

Windows 98 closes the Windows Help window.

Shutting Down Windows 98

After completing your work with Windows 98, you may want to shut down Windows 98 using the **Shut Down command** on the Start menu. If you are sure you want to shut down Windows 98, perform the following steps. If you are not sure about shutting down Windows 98, read the following steps without actually performing them.

 To Shut Down Windows 98

1. **Click the Start button on the taskbar and then point to Shut Down on the Start menu (Figure 1-50).**

> **More About**
>
> **Shut Down Procedures**
>
> Some users of Windows 98 have turned off their computers without following the shut down procedure only to find data they thought they had stored on disk was lost. Because of the way Windows 98 writes data on the disk, it is important you shut down Windows properly so you do not lose your work.

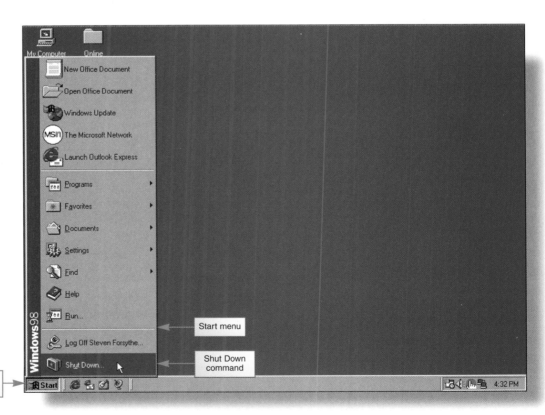

FIGURE 1-50

2 **Click Shut Down. Point to the OK button in the Shut Down Windows dialog box.**

The desktop darkens and the Shut Down Windows dialog box displays (Figure 1-51). The dialog box contains three option buttons. The selected option button, Shut down, indicates that clicking the OK button will shut down Windows 98.

3 **Click the OK button.**

Windows 98 is shut down.

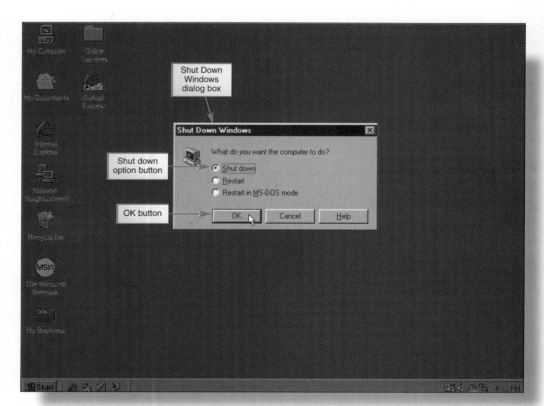

FIGURE 1-51

Other Ways

1. Press CTRL+ESC, press U, Press UP ARROW or DOWN ARROW key to select Shut down option button, press ENTER

2. Press ALT+F4, press UP ARROW or DOWN ARROW key to select Shut down option button, press ENTER

Two screens display while Windows 98 is shutting down. The first screen containing the Windows logo, Windows 98 name, and the text, Windows is shutting down, displays momentarily while Windows 98 is being shut down. Then, a second screen containing the text, It's now safe to turn off your computer, displays. At this point you can turn off your computer. When shutting down Windows 98, you should never turn off your computer before these two screens display.

If you accidentally click Shut Down on the Start menu and you do not want to shut down Windows 98, click the Cancel button in the Shut Down Windows dialog box to return to normal Windows 98 operation.

Project Summary

Project 1 illustrated the Microsoft Windows 98 graphical user interface. You started Windows 98, learned the parts of the desktop, and learned to point, click, right-click, double-click, drag, and right-drag. You learned about the Internet World Wide Web, the three desktop views (Classic, Web, and Custom), and launched an application. Using both the Help Content and the Help Index sheets you obtained Help about Microsoft Windows 98. You shut down Windows 98 using the Shut Down command on the Start menu.

What You Should Know

Having completed this project, you now should be able to perform the following tasks:

▶ Close a Window *(WIN 1.24)*

▶ Close a Window and Reopen a Window *(WIN 1.19)*

▶ Close the Welcome Screen *(WIN 1.8)*

▶ Close Windows Help *(WIN 1.41)*

▶ Launch a Program Using an Icon on the Desktop *(WIN 1.35)*

▶ Launch a Program Using the Quick Launch Toolbar *(WIN 1.34)*

▶ Launch a Program Using the Start Menu *(WIN 1.32)*

▶ Launch Windows Help *(WIN 1.36)*

▶ Maximize and Restore a Window *(WIN 1.17)*

▶ Minimize and Redisplay a Window *(WIN 1.15)*

▶ Move an Object by Dragging *(WIN 1.20)*

▶ Open a Window by Double-Clicking *(WIN 1.13)*

▶ Point and Click *(WIN 1.9)*

▶ Resize a Window *(WIN 1.24)*

▶ Right-Click *(WIN 1.12)*

▶ Right-Drag *(WIN 1.25)*

▶ Scroll a Window Using Scroll Arrows *(WIN 1.22)*

▶ Shut Down Windows 98 *(WIN 1.41)*

▶ Size a Window by Dragging *(WIN 1.21)*

▶ Use Help to Find a Topic in Help *(WIN 1.37)*

▶ Use the Help Index Sheet *(WIN 1.39)*

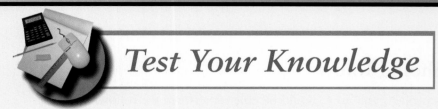

Test Your Knowledge

1 True/False

Instructions: Circle T if the statement is true or F if the statement is false.

T F 1. A user interface is a combination of computer hardware and computer software.

T F 2. The Quick Launch toolbar displays on the taskbar at the bottom of the desktop.

T F 3. Click means press the right mouse button.

T F 4. When you drag an object on the desktop, Windows 98 displays a shortcut menu.

T F 5. Double-clicking the My Computer icon on the desktop opens a window.

T F 6. You can maximize a window by dragging the title bar of the window.

T F 7. Viewing the desktop in Web style causes the desktop and the objects on the desktop to display and function as they did in Windows 95.

T F 8. One of the basic tasks you can perform using the Windows 98 operating system is to launch an application program.

T F 9. You can launch Windows Help by clicking the Start button and then clicking Help on the Start menu.

T F 10. To find an entry in the Windows Help Index, type the first few characters of the entry in the text box in the Contents sheet.

2 Multiple Choice

Instructions: Circle the correct response.

1. Through a user interface, the user is able to _____.
   a. control the computer
   b. request information from the computer
   c. respond to messages displayed by the computer
   d. all of the above

2. A shortcut menu opens when you _____ a(n) _____.
   a. right-click, object
   b. click, menu name on the menu bar
   c. click, submenu
   d. click, recessed button in the taskbar button area

3. In this book, a dark blue title bar and a recessed button in the taskbar button area indicate a window is _____.
   a. inactive
   b. minimized
   c. closed
   d. active

Test Your Knowledge

4. To view the contents of a window that are not currently visible in the window, use the _____.
   a. title bar
   b. scroll bar
   c. menu bar
   d. Restore button

5. _____ is holding down the right mouse button, moving an item to the desired location, and then releasing the right mouse button.
   a. Double-clicking
   b. Right-clicking
   c. Right-dragging
   d. Pointing

6. Text that is underlined in a browser window is called a(n) _____.
   a. uniform resource locator
   b. hyperlink
   c. hypertext document
   d. Web page

7. When the desktop is viewed in Web style, the icons on the desktop are _____ and the _____ Desktop displays.
   a. underlined, Active
   b. not underlined, Active
   c. underlined, Classic Windows
   d. not underlined, Classic Windows

8. Which method cannot be used to launch the Internet Explorer application?
   a. Click the Start button, point to Programs, point to Internet Explorer, and click Internet Explorer.
   b. Click the Launch Internet Explorer Browser icon on the Quick Launch toolbar.
   c. Click the Internet Explorer channel button on the Internet Explorer Channel bar.
   d. Click the Internet Explorer icon on the desktop.

9. For information about an index entry on the Index sheet of the Windows Help window, click the Help topic and _____.
   a. press the F1 key
   b. click the Forward button on the toolbar
   c. click the Search tab
   d. click the Display button

10. To shut down Windows 98, _____.
    a. click the Start button, click Shut Down, and click the OK button
    b. click File on the menu bar and then click Shut Down
    c. right-click the taskbar, click Shut down on the shortcut menu, and click the OK button
    d. press the F10 key and then click the OK button

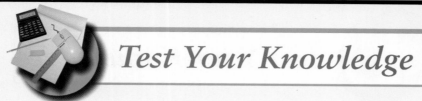

Test Your Knowledge

3 Identifying the Objects on the Desktop

Instructions: On the desktop shown in Figure 1-52, arrows point to several items or objects on the desktop. Identify the items or objects in the spaces provided.

4. _____

5. _____

6. _____

7. _____

8. _____

9. _____

10. _____

11. _____

14. _____

3. _____

2. _____

1. _____

12. _____

13. _____

New Office Document
Open Office Document
Windows Update
The Microsoft Network
Launch Outlook Express
Programs
Favorites
Documents
Settings
Find
Help
Run...
Log Off Steven Forsythe...
Shut Down...

My Computer

File   Edit   View

Back   Forward   Up   Cut   Copy   Paste

3½ Floppy (A:)   Hard disk (C:)   (D:)   Removable Disk (E:)   (F:)

Printers   Control Panel   Dial-Up Networking   Scheduled Tasks

9 object(s)   My Computer

Start   My Computer   4:34 PM

FIGURE 1-52

4 Launching the Internet Explorer Browser

Instructions: In the space provided, list the steps for the three methods used in this project to launch the Internet Explorer browser.

Method 1:

Step 1: _____

Step 2: _____

Step 3: _____

Step 4: _____

Method 2:

Step 1: _____

Method 3:

Step 1: _____

Use Help

1 Using Windows Help

Instructions: Use Windows Help and a computer to perform the following tasks.

Part 1: *Using the Question Mark Button*

1. If necessary, start Microsoft Windows 98. Click the Start button on the taskbar. Point to Settings on the Start menu. Click Folder Options on the Settings submenu.
2. Click the General tab in the Folder Options dialog box. A dialog box displays whenever Windows 98 needs to supply information to you or requires you to enter information or select among several options.
3. Click the question mark button on the title bar. The mouse pointer changes to a block arrow with question mark.
4. Click the preview monitor in the General sheet. A pop-up window displays explaining the contents of the preview monitor. Read the information in the pop-up window.
5. Click an open area of the General sheet to remove the pop-up window.
6. Click the question mark button on the title bar and then click the Web style option button. A pop-up window displays explaining what happens when you select this option. Read the information in the pop-up window.
7. Click the question mark button on the title bar and then click the Classic style option button. A pop-up window displays explaining what happens when you select this option. Read the information in the pop-up window.
8. Click the question mark button on the title bar and then click the Custom, based on settings you choose option button. A pop-up window displays explaining what happens when you select this option. Read the information in the pop-up window.
9. Click the question mark button on the title bar and then click the Settings button. A pop-up window displays explaining the function of the button. Read the information in the pop-up window.
10. Click an open area of the General sheet to remove the pop-up window.
11. Summarize the function of the question mark button. _____
12. Click the Close button in the Folder Options dialog box.

Part 2: *Finding What's New in Windows 98*

1. Click the Start button and then click Help on the Start menu.
2. Click the Maximize button on Windows Help title bar.
3. If the Contents sheet does not display, click the Contents tab. Click the Introducing Windows 98 closed book icon.
4. Click the What's New in Windows 98 closed book icon.
5. Click the True Web integration Help topic. Seven hyperlinks display in the right frame.
6. Click the Active Desktop hyperlink in the right frame and read the information about the Active Desktop.
7. Click the Channels hyperlink and read the information about channels.
8. Click the Options button on the Help toolbar to display the Options menu and then click Print.
9. Click the OK button in the Print dialog box to print the True Web integration screen.

(continued)

Use Help

Using Windows Help *(continued)*

Part 3: *Reading About the Online Getting Started Manual*

1. Click the Getting Started Book: Online Version closed book icon in the left frame.
2. Click the Microsoft Windows 98 Getting Started Book Help topic. Read the information Windows 98 displays about the Getting Started Book in the right frame. The *Getting Started Book* is the printed manual for Windows 98.
3. Click the Click here hyperlink in the right frame to open the Getting Started window.
4. If the Contents sheet does not display, click the Contents tab. Click the Introducing Getting Started closed book icon. Click and read each of the four Help topics that display.
5. Click the Welcome closed book icon. Three Help topics and two closed book icons display in the open book. Click and read the Overview, Windows 98 at a Glance, and If You're New to Windows topics.
6. Click the Where to Find Information closed book icon.
7. Click the Resources Included with Windows 98 closed book icon. Click and read the Overview topic.
8. Click the Online Tutorial: Discover Windows 98 topic. Read the information about the topic.
9. Click the Troubleshooters topic. Read the information about the topic.
10. Click the Back button on the Help toolbar to display the previous screen (Online Tutorial: Discover Windows 98) in the right frame.
11. Click the Options button on the Help toolbar, click Print, and click the OK button to print the Help topic.
12. Click the Close button in the Getting Started window.
13. Click the Close button in the Windows Help window.

2 Using Windows Help to Obtain Help

Instructions: Use Windows Help and a computer to perform the following tasks.

1. Find Help about viewing the Welcome to Windows 98 screen that displays when you launch Windows 98. Use the search word, welcome, and the Index sheet. Answer the following questions in the spaces provided.
   a. How can you open the Welcome to Windows 98 screen? _____
   b. Open the Welcome to Windows 98 screen. How many entries does the Contents menu contain?

   _____
   c. Point to Discover Windows 98 on the Contents menu. What are the three choices available in Discover Windows 98? _____
   d. Point to Maintain Your Computer on the Contents menu. How can using Maintain Your Computer benefit your computer? _____
   e. Close the Welcome to Windows 98 screen.
2. Find Help about keyboard shortcuts by looking in the Exploring Your Computer book. Answer the following questions in the spaces provided.
   a. What keyboard shortcut is used to close the current window or quit a program?

   _____
   b. What keyboard shortcut is used to display the Start menu? _____

Use Help

c. What keyboard shortcut is used to display the shortcut menu for a selected item?
   _____

d. What keyboard shortcut is used to rename an item? _____

e. What keyboard shortcut is used to view an item's properties? _____

3. Find Help about changing the Windows Help window by looking in the Introducing Windows 98 book. Answer the following questions in the spaces provided.
   a. How do you hide the Contents, Index, and Search tabs? _____
   b. How do you make the left frame larger? _____
   c. Which software application do you use to change the color or fonts in the Help window?
      _____

4. Find Help about the desktop by looking in the Windows Desktop book in the Exploring Your Computer book. Answer the following questions in the spaces provided.
   a. What does the Active Desktop allow you to do? _____
   b. What does the Address toolbar enable you do? _____
   c. What commands do you use to find a person on the Internet? _____

5. Find Help about what to do if you have a problem in Windows 98. The process of solving such a problem is called _____. Answer the following questions in the spaces provided.
   a. What should you check if only part of a document prints on your printer?
      _____
   b. What could the problem be if Windows 98 does not detect that you have a modem connected to your computer?" _____
   c. What could the problem be if the computer restarts each time a sound is played?
      _____

6. Using the Index sheet in the Windows Help window, answer the following questions in the space provided.
   a. How do you get Help in a dialog box? _____
   b. What dialog box do you use to change the appearance of the mouse pointer?
      _____
   c. How do you minimize all open windows? _____
   d. How do you hide the Internet Explorer Channel bar? _____

7. Obtain information on software licensing by answering the following questions. Find and then print information from Windows Help that supports your answers.
   a. How does the law protect computer software? _____
   b. What is software piracy? _____ Why should I be concerned about it?
      _____
   c. What is an EULA (end user licensing agreement)? _____
   d. Can you use your own software on both your desktop and your laptop computers?
      _____
   e. How can you identify illegal software? _____

(continued)

Use Help

Using Windows Help to Obtain Help *(continued)*

8. Your best friend just bought a new computer. Among the software packages she obtained when she received the computer was a NHL hockey game from Microsoft. She has no interest in hockey but she knows you are an avid hockey fan. Answer the following questions and then print the information supporting your answers from Windows Help. Can she legally give this software to you? _____ Can she legally sell this software to you to help recover some of her costs? _____ Can she give you the software and still keep the hockey game on her computer for use by another member of her family? _____

9. Close all open windows.

In the Lab

1 Improving Your Mouse Skills

Instructions: Use a computer to perform the following tasks:

1. Start Microsoft Windows 98 if necessary.
2. Click the Start button on the taskbar, point to Programs on the Start menu, point to Accessories on the Programs submenu, point to Games on the Accessories submenu, and click Solitaire on the Games submenu.
3. Click the Maximize button in the Solitaire window.
4. Click Help on the Solitaire menu bar and then click Help Topics.
5. If the Contents sheet does not display, click the Contents tab.
6. Review the Playing Solitaire and Choosing a scoring system topics in the Contents sheet.
7. After reviewing the Help topics, close all Help windows.
8. Play the game of Solitaire.
9. Click the Close button on the Solitaire title bar to close the game.

In the Lab

2 **Using the Discover Windows 98 Tutorial**

Instructions: To use the Discover Windows 98 tutorial you will need a copy of the Windows 98 CD-ROM. If this CD-ROM is not available, skip this lab assignment. Otherwise, use a computer and the CD-ROM to perform the following tasks:

1. Start Microsoft Windows 98 if necessary.
2. Insert the Windows 98 CD-ROM in your CD-ROM drive. If the Windows 98 CD-ROM window displays, click the Close button in the window to close the window.
3. Click the Start button on the taskbar, point to Programs on the Start menu, point to Accessories on the Programs submenu, point to System Tools on the Accessories submenu, and click Welcome to Windows on the System Tools submenu.
4. Click Discover Windows 98 in the Welcome to Windows 98 window to display the Discover Windows 98 Contents.
5. Click the Computer Essentials title (hyperlink) in the right panel of the Discover Windows 98 Contents screen. The Computer Essentials tutorial starts and fills the desktop. The left panel contains a list of lessons. A left arrow to the right of a lesson indicates the current lesson. Pressing the RIGHT ARROW key on the keyboard displays the next screen in the lesson. Pressing the UP ARROW key quits the Computer Essentials tutorial. Clicking the Contents button displays the Table of Contents in the Discover Windows 98 Contents screen.
6. Press the RIGHT ARROW key to begin the Introduction.
7. When appropriate, press the number 1 key to begin the Meeting Your Computer section. Complete this lesson. This lesson takes approximately ten minutes.
8. Click the Contents button to display the Discover Windows 98 Contents screen.
9. If you have experience using Windows 3.0 or Windows 3.1 and are learning to use Windows 98, click the Windows 98 Overview title. Otherwise, go to Step 10. This lesson takes approximately ten minutes.
10. If you have experience using Windows 95 and are learning to use Windows 98, click the What's New title. Otherwise, go to Step 11. Press any key on the keyboard to begin the lesson. Features are organized into five groups. Click each feature (hyperlink) in each group to view a demonstration. When finished, click the Exit button. This lesson takes approximately twenty minutes.
11. If time permits, click the More Windows 98 Resources title. Click the Microsoft Windows 98 Starts Here title (1) and then click the Microsoft Press title (2) to view additional information about Windows 98. Click each of the three hyperlinks below the Resources title to explore three Windows-related Web sites. When finished, click the Close button in the Microsoft Internet Explorer window and click the Contents button.
12. Click the Close button in the Discover Windows 98 Contents screen.
13. Click the Yes button in the Discover Windows 98 dialog box.
14. Click the Close button in the Welcome to Windows 98 window.
15. Remove the Windows 98 CD-ROM from your CD-ROM drive.

In the Lab

3 Launching and Using the Internet Explorer Application

Instructions: Perform the following steps to launch the Internet Explorer application.

Part 1: *Launching the Internet Explorer Application*

1. Start Microsoft Windows 98 and, if necessary, connect to the Internet.
2. Click the Internet Explorer icon on the Quick Launch toolbar.
3. If the Address bar does not display below the Standard Buttons toolbar in the Microsoft Internet Explorer window, click View on the menu bar, point to Toolbars, and click Address Bar on the Toolbars submenu.

Part 2: *Entering a URL in the Address Bar*

1. Click the URL in the Address bar to highlight the URL.
2. Type http://www.microsoft.com in the Address bar and press the ENTER key.
3. What URL displays in the Address bar? _____ What window title displays in the title bar? _____
4. Scroll the Web page to view the contents of the Web page. List two topics that are shown on this Web page. _____ List five hyperlinks (underlined text) that are shown on this Web page. _____
5. Click any hyperlink on the Web page. What hyperlink did you click? _____
6. Describe the Web page that displayed when you clicked the hyperlink? _____
7. Click the Print button on the Standard Buttons toolbar to print the Web page.

Part 3: *Entering a URL in the Address Bar*

1. Click the URL in the Address bar to highlight the URL.
2. Type http://www.disney.com in the Address bar and press the ENTER key.
3. What window title displays in the title bar? _____
4. Scroll the Web page to view the contents of the Web page. Do any graphic images display on the Web page? _____ If so, describe two images. _____
5. Pointing to an image on a Web page and having the mouse pointer change to a hand indicates the image is a hyperlink. Does the Web page include an image that is a hyperlink? _____ If so, describe the image. _____
6. Click the hyperlink to display another Web page. What window title displays in the title bar? _____
7. Click the Print button on the Standard Buttons toolbar to print the Web page.

Part 4: *Displaying Previously Displayed Web Pages*

1. Click the Back button on the Standard Buttons toolbar. What Web page displays? _____
2. Click the Back button on the Standard Buttons toolbar twice. What Web page displays? _____
3. Click the Forward button on the Standard Buttons toolbar bar. What Web page displays? _____

In the Lab

Part 5: *Entering a URL in the Address Bar*

1. Click the URL in the Address bar to highlight the URL.
2. Type http://www.scsite.com/WIN98/ in the Address bar and press the ENTER key.
3. Click the Steve's Cool Sites hyperlink on the Web page.
4. Click any hyperlinks that are of interest to you. Which hyperlink did you like the best? _____
5. Use the Back or Forward button to display the Web site you like the best.
6. Click the Print button on the Standard Buttons toolbar to print the Web page.
7. Click the Close button on the Microsoft Internet Explorer title bar.

4 Launching an Application

Instructions:

Perform the following steps to launch the Notepad application using the Start menu, and create the daily reminders list shown in Figure 1-53. **Notepad** is a popular application program available with Windows 98 that allows you to create, save, and print simple text documents.

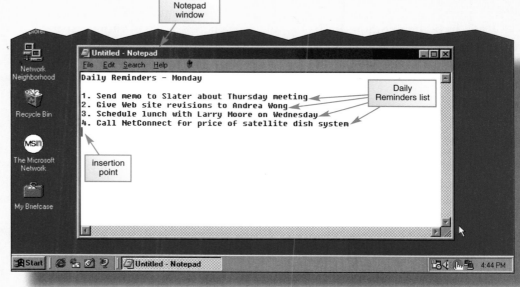

FIGURE 1-53

1. Start Microsoft Windows 98 if necessary.
2. Click the Start button. Point to Programs on the Start menu, point to Accessories on the Programs submenu, and click Notepad on the Accessories submenu. The Untitled - Notepad window displays and an insertion point (flashing vertical line) displays in the blank area below the menu bar.
3. Type Daily Reminders - Monday and press the ENTER key twice.
4. Type 1. Send memo to Slater about Thursday meeting and press the ENTER key.
5. Type 2. Give Web site revisions to Andrea Wong and press the ENTER key.
6. Type 3. Schedule lunch with Larry Moore on Wednesday and press the ENTER key.
7. Type 4. Call NetConnect for prices of satellite dish system and press the ENTER key.
8. Click File on the menu bar and then click Print.
9. Retrieve the printed Daily Reminders list from the printer.
10. Click the Close button on the Notepad title bar.
11. Click the No button in the Notepad dialog box to not save the Daily Reminders document.

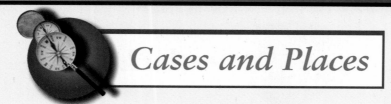

Cases and Places

The difficulty of these case studies varies:
❘ are the least difficult; ❘❘ are more difficult; and ❘❘❘ are the most difficult.

1 ❘ Using Windows Help, locate the Getting Started Online Manual. Using the Online Manual read about the following ten topics: Connecting to a Network, Customizing Your Desktop, Emergency Startup Disk, FAT32 File, System Explorer Bars, Microsoft NetMeeting, My Documents Folder, OnNow Power Management, TDD Service, and Watching TV. Select five of the ten topics. In a brief report, summarize the five topics you have selected.

2 ❘ Technical support is an important consideration when installing and using an operating system or an application software program. The ability to obtain a valid answer to your question at the moment you have the question can be the difference between a frustrating experience and a positive experience. Using Windows 98 Help, the Internet, or another research facility, write a brief report on the options that are available for obtaining help and technical support while using Windows 98.

3 ❘❘ Microsoft's decision to make the Internet Explorer 4 Web browser part of the Windows 98 operating system caused many legal problems for Microsoft. Using the Internet, computer magazines and newspapers, or other resources, prepare a brief report on these legal problems. Explain the arguments for and against combining the browser and operating system. Identify the key players on both sides of the legal battle and summarize the final decision. Did the legal process or final decision affect the release date and contents of Windows 98? Do you think computer users benefited from this decision? Explain your answers.

4 ❘❘❘ Because of the many important tasks an operating system performs, most businesses put a great deal of thought into choosing an operating system for their personal computers. Interview a person at a local business on the operating system it uses with its personal computers. Based on your interview, write a brief report on why the business chose that operating system, how satisfied it is with it, and under what circumstances it might consider switching to a different operating system.

5 ❘❘❘ In addition to Windows 98, Microsoft also sells the Windows NT operating system. Some say Windows NT will replace Windows 98 in the future. Using the Internet, computer magazines, or other resources, prepare a brief report comparing and contrasting the operating systems. How do their graphical user interfaces compare? What features and commands are shared by both operating systems? Does either operating system have features or commands that the other operating system does not have? Explain whether you think Windows NT could replace Windows 98.

Microsoft Windows 98

Using Windows Explorer

P R O J E C T

You will have mastered the material in this project when you can:

O B J E C T I V E S

- Start Windows Explorer
- Identify the elements of the Exploring – My Computer window
- Display the contents of a folder
- Expand and collapse a folder
- Change the view
- Select and copy one file or a group of files
- Create, rename, and delete a folder
- Rename and delete a file

MOORE
AND
More Storage

Cramming Data in Small Places

Is it any doubt that you are an expert when it comes to cramming? You cram for final exams, cram books into heavy backpacks, and cram clothes into tiny closets. Only a few decades ago, college students held contests to see how many people could cram into telephone booths and Volkswagen Beetles. About the same time, Gordon Moore, a semiconductor engineer, realized cramming was a good thing when it came to computer chips.

In 1965, Moore observed a trend when he was drawing an illustration for a speech: every 18 to 24 months a new memory chip was being released with double the number of transistors as its predecessor. He predicted that this growth would continue exponentially, and he was correct. Today's Pentium II processor has 7.5 million transistors, which is nearly 3,200 times more than the 2,300 transistors found on a chip released in 1971.

7.5 MILLION

His theory became known as Moore's Law. In 1968, Gordon Moore became a cofounder of Intel Corporation, one of the world's largest microprocessor manufacturers.

Hard disk capacity has grown to impressive densities in recent years. In 1956, IBM's first hard drive stored five megabytes (five million bytes) of data. Subsequent drive capacity doubled every 30 months until 1991. At that time, IBM introduced new technology that doubled capacity every 18 months. IBM needed a truck to deliver that refrigerator-sized first hard drive, which consisted of fifty 24-inch disks, called platters, and cost more than $1 million, at the value of today's dollars. The hard drive in your computer probably has two 3½-inch platters, stores at least four gigabytes (four billion bytes), and costs less than $300.

With such increased disk capacity, computers store more data, programs, and files than ever before. Consider how in this project, you will manage and organize files and documents using tools supplied with Windows 98. You will master the operations of copying, moving, renaming, and deleting files stored on your computer's floppy disk and then display your computer's hard disk properties. Do you wonder how all the data files and programs fit on those disks?

Engineers use the term, *areal density,* when referring to capacity, which is a combination of the disk's magnetic properties, read/write head movement, and electronic principles. As the hard disk's platters whirl at 3,600 to 7,200 revolutions per minute, read/write heads attached to access arms move to the correct position on a particular platter and retrieve or record bits of data.

Technology gurus predict that Moore's Law for silicon chips will hold true until 2020. At that time, they will be forced to use new methods and materials, such as the optical technique of holography. As for disk drives, capacity may max out in 2010, when densities will reach 70 to 100 gigabytes per square inch, as compared with today's one gigabyte per square inch. Engineers are investigating holographic storage, which will hold 1,000 gigabytes per square inch, but they have set their sights on technologies that could lead to capacities of one million gigabytes per square inch.

With that capacity in your computer, just think of how many programs and data files you will be able to cram into that space. Be forewarned: you probably will need every bit (or byte) of this space to hold the progressive applications planned for the next decade and beyond.

Microsoft Windows 98

Using Windows Explorer

PROJECT

2

C A S E   P E R S P E C T I V E

Your organization has decided to switch to Windows 98 from Windows 95. Your supervisor has read in computer magazines that to use Windows 98 effectively, people must learn Windows 98 Explorer. Although almost everyone is excited about the change, those who have little experience using Windows 98 are apprehensive about having to learn about file management. You have been asked to teach a class with an emphasis on file management to all employees who are not experienced Windows users. Your goal in Project 2 is to become competent using Windows Explorer so you can teach the class.

Introduction

Windows Explorer is an application program included with Windows 98 that allows you to view the contents of the computer, the hierarchy of folders on the computer, and the files and folders in each folder.

Windows Explorer also allows you to organize the files and folders on the computer by copying and moving the files and folders. In this project, you will use Windows Explorer to (1) work with the files and folders on your computer; (2) select and copy a group of files between the hard drive and a floppy disk; (3) create, rename, and delete a folder on a floppy disk; and (4) rename and delete a file on a floppy disk. These are common operations that you should understand how to perform.

Starting Windows 98

As explained in Project 1, when you turn on the computer, an introductory screen consisting of the Windows logo and Windows name displays on a blue sky and clouds background. The screen clears and Windows 98 displays several items on the desktop.

If the Welcome to Windows 98 screen displays on your desktop, click the Close button on the title bar to close the screen. Nine icons (My Computer, My Documents, Internet Explorer, Network Neighborhood, Recycle Bin, The Microsoft Network, My Briefcase, Online Services, and Outlook Express) display along the left edge of the desktop and the taskbar displays along the bottom of the desktop (Figure 2-1).

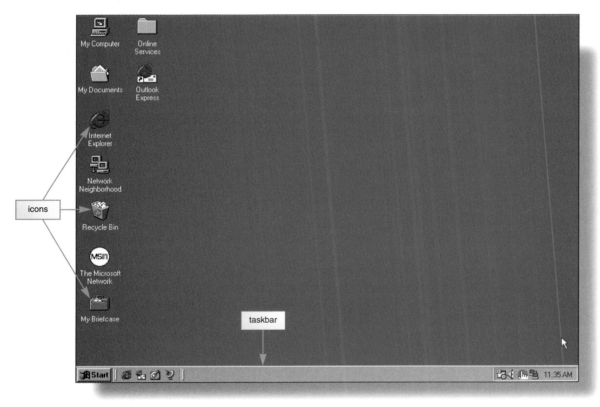

FIGURE 2-1

Starting Windows Explorer and Maximizing Its Window

To explore the files and folders on the computer, start Windows Explorer and maximize its window by performing the steps on the next page.

Microsoft **Windows 98**

 Steps ## To Start Windows Explorer and Maximize Its Window

1 **Right-click the My Computer icon on the desktop and then point to Explore on the shortcut menu.**

The My Computer icon is highlighted, a shortcut menu displays, and the Explore command is highlighted (Figure 2-2).

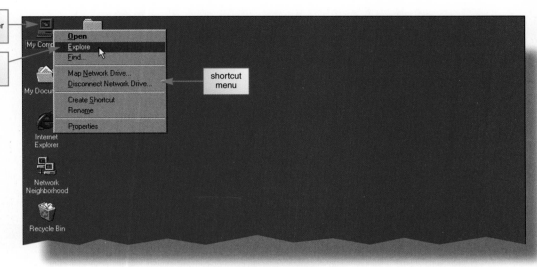

FIGURE 2-2

2 **Click Explore and then click the Maximize button on the Exploring – My Computer title bar.**

The Exploring – My Computer window opens and is maximized. The recessed Exploring – My Computer button is added to the taskbar button area (Figure 2-3).

Other Ways

1. Right-click Start button, click Explore on shortcut menu
2. Click Start button, point to Programs, click Windows Explorer
3. Right-click any icon on desktop (except The Microsoft Network icon and Outlook Express icon), click Explore on shortcut menu
4. Right-click Start button or any icon on desktop except The Microsoft Network icon and Outlook Express icon, press E

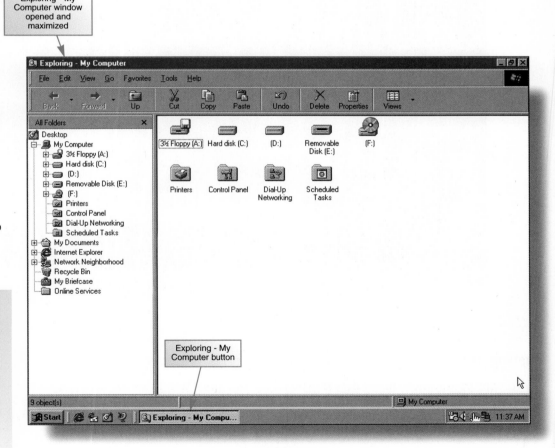

FIGURE 2-3

Windows Explorer

When you start Windows Explorer by right-clicking the My Computer icon, Windows 98 opens the Exploring – My Computer window (Figure 2-4). The menu bar contains the File, Edit, View, Go, Favorites, Tools, and Help menu names. These menus contain commands to organize and work with the drives on the computer and the files and folders on those drives. Below the menu bar is the Standard Buttons toolbar.

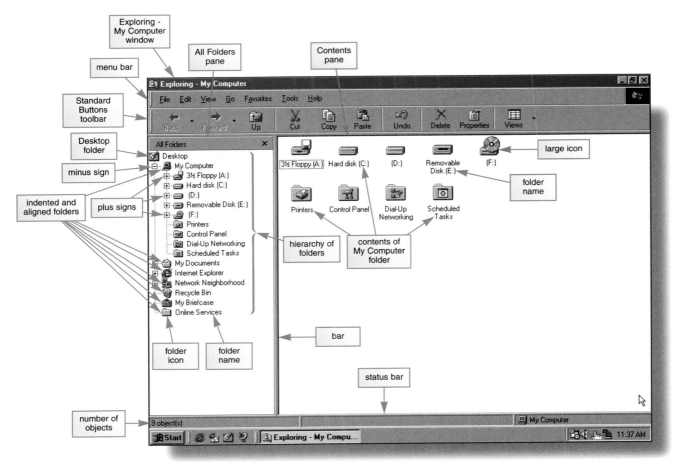

FIGURE 2-4

The main window is divided into two panes separated by a bar. The left pane of the window, identified by the All Folders title, contains a **hierarchy** of folders on the computer. The right pane of the window displays the contents of the My Computer folder. In Figure 2-4, the Contents pane contains the icons and folder names of nine folders (3½ Floppy (A:), Hard disk (C:), (D:), Removable Disk (E:), (F:), Printers, Control Panel, Dial-Up Networking, and Scheduled Tasks). These folders may be different on your computer. You can change the size of the All Folders and Contents panes by dragging the bar that separates the two panes.

Each folder in the All Folders pane is represented by an icon and folder name. The first folder, consisting of an icon and the Desktop folder name, represents the desktop of the computer. The seven folders indented and aligned below the Desktop folder name (My Computer, My Documents, Internet Explorer, Network Neighborhood, Recycle Bin, My Briefcase, and Online Services) are connected to the vertical line below the Desktop icon. These folders correspond to seven of the nine icons displayed on the left edge of the desktop (see Figure 2-1 on page WIN 2.5). These folders may be different on your computer.

Windows 98 displays a minus sign (–) in a box to the left of an icon in the All Folders pane to indicate the corresponding folder contains one or more folders that are visible in the All Folders pane. These folders, called **subfolders**, are indented and aligned below the folder name.

In Figure 2-4 on the previous page, a minus sign precedes the My Computer icon, and nine subfolders are indented and display below the My Computer folder name. The nine subfolders (3½ Floppy (A:), Hard disk (C:), (D:), Removable Disk (E:), (F:), Printers, Control Panel, Dial-Up Networking, and Scheduled Tasks) correspond to the nine folders in the Contents pane. Clicking the minus sign, referred to as **collapsing the folder**, removes the indented subfolders from the hierarchy of folders in the All Folders pane and changes the minus sign to a plus sign.

Windows 98 displays a plus sign (+) in a box to the left of an icon to indicate the corresponding folder consists of one or more subfolders that are not visible in the All Folders pane. In Figure 2-4, a plus sign precedes the first five icons indented and aligned below the My Computer name (3½ Floppy (A:), Hard disk (C:), (D:), Removable (E:), and (F:) icons). Clicking the plus sign, referred to as **expanding the folder**, displays a list of indented subfolders and changes the plus sign to a minus sign.

If neither a plus sign nor a minus sign displays to the left of an icon, the folder does not contain subfolders. In Figure 2-4 on the previous page, the Printers, Control Panel, Dial-Up Networking, Scheduled Tasks, Recycle Bin, My Briefcase, and Online Services icons are not preceded by a plus or minus sign and do not contain subfolders.

The status bar at the bottom of the Exploring – My Computer window indicates the number of folders, or objects, displayed in the Contents pane of the window (9 object(s)). Depending on the objects displayed in the Contents pane, the amount of disk space the objects occupy and the amount of unused disk space also may display on the status bar. If the status bar does not display in the Exploring – My Computer window on your computer, click View on the menu bar and then click the Status Bar.

In addition to using Windows Explorer to explore your computer by right-clicking the My Computer icon, you also can use Windows Explorer to explore different aspects of your computer by right-clicking the Start button on the taskbar and the My Documents, Internet Explorer, Network Neighborhood, Recycle Bin, My Briefcase, and Online Services icons on the desktop.

Displaying the Contents of a Folder

In Figure 2-4 on the previous page, the Contents pane contains the subfolders in the My Computer folder. In addition to displaying the contents of the My Computer folder, the contents of any folder in the All Folders pane can be displayed in the Contents pane. Perform the following steps to display the contents of the Hard disk (C:) folder.

Steps **To Display the Contents of a Folder**

1 Point to the Hard
disk (C:) folder
name in the All Folders
pane of the Exploring –
My Computer window
(Figure 2-5).

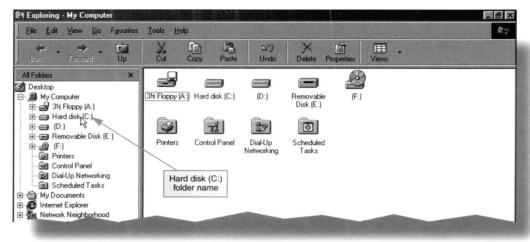

FIGURE 2-5

2 Click the Hard disk
(C:) folder name.

*The highlighted Hard disk
(C:) folder name displays
in the All Folders pane, the
contents of the Hard
disk (C:) folder
display in the
Contents pane, the window
title and button in the taskbar
button area change to reflect
the folder name, and the
messages on the status bar
change (Figure 2-6).*

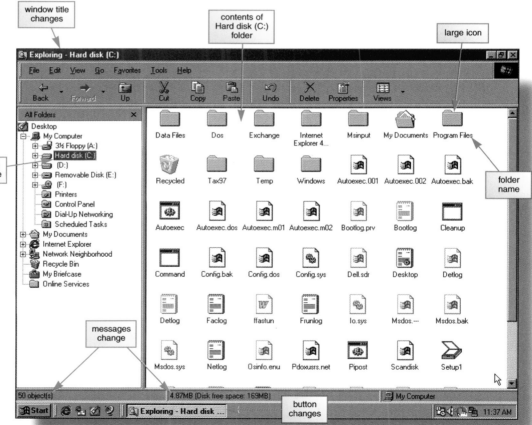

FIGURE 2-6

The status bar messages shown in Figure 2-6 indicate 50 objects, the objects
occupy 4.87MB of disk space, and the amount of unused (free) disk space is 169MB.
The contents of the Hard disk (C:) folder may be different on your computer.

Other Ways

1. Double-click Hard disk (C:)
   icon in Contents pane
2. Press TAB to select any icon
   in All Folders pane, press
   DOWN ARROW or UP ARROW to
   select Hard disk (C:) icon in
   Contents pane

In addition to displaying the contents of the Hard disk (C:) folder, you can display the contents of the other folders by clicking the corresponding icon or folder name in the All Folders pane. The contents of the folder you click then will display in the Contents pane of the window.

Expanding a Folder

Currently, the Hard disk (C:) folder is highlighted in the All Folders pane of the Exploring – Hard disk (C:) window, and the contents of the Hard disk (C:) folder display in the Contents pane. Windows 98 displays a plus sign (+) to the left of the Hard disk (C:) icon to indicate the folder contains subfolders that are not visible in the hierarchy of folders in the All Folders pane. To expand the Hard disk (C:) folder and display its subfolders, perform the following steps.

 To Expand a Folder

1 **Point to the plus sign to the left of the Hard disk (C:) icon in the All Folders pane (Figure 2-7).**

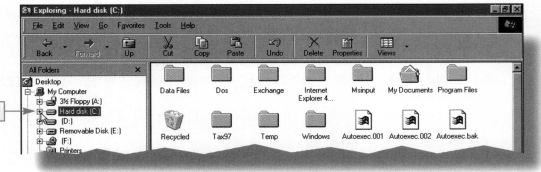

FIGURE 2-7

2 **Click the plus sign to display the subfolders in the Hard disk (C:) folder.**

A minus sign replaces the plus sign preceding the Hard disk (C:) icon, a vertical scroll bar displays, and the Hard disk (C:) folder expands (Figure 2-8). The window title and the files and folders in the Contents pane remain unchanged.

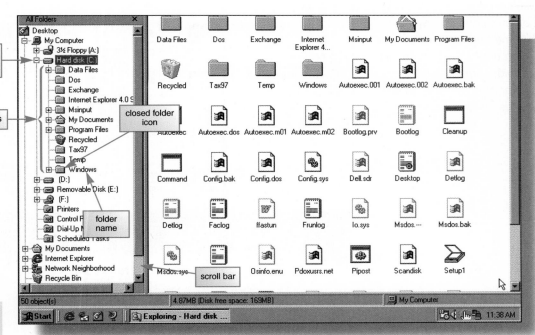

FIGURE 2-8

Other **Ways**

1. Double-click the folder icon
2. Select folder icon, press PLUS SIGN on numeric keypad (or RIGHT ARROW)

The subfolders in the expanded Hard disk (C:) folder shown in Figure 2-8 are indented and aligned below the Hard disk (C:) folder name. A closed folder icon and folder name identify each subfolder in the Hard disk (C:) folder.

Collapsing a Folder

Currently, the subfolders in the Hard disk (C:) folder display indented and aligned below the Hard disk (C:) folder name (see Figure 2-8). Windows 98 displays a minus sign (–) to the left of the Hard disk (C:) icon to indicate the folder is expanded. To collapse the Hard disk (C:) folder and then remove its subfolders from the hierarchy of folders in the All Folders pane, perform the following steps.

 To Collapse a Folder

1 **Point to the minus sign preceding the Hard disk (C:) icon in the All Folders pane (Figure 2-9).**

FIGURE 2-9

2 **Click the minus sign to display the Hard disk (C:) folder without its subfolders.**

A plus sign replaces the minus sign preceding the Hard disk (C:) icon and the subfolders in the Hard disk (C:) folder are removed from the hierarchy of folders (Figure 2-10).

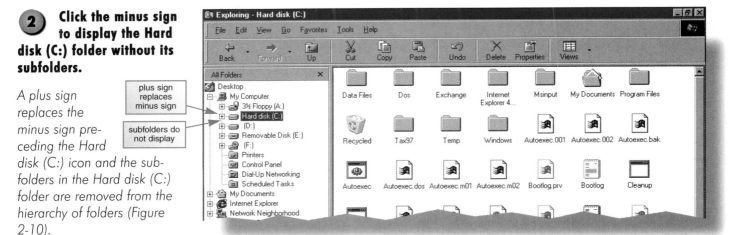

FIGURE 2-10

Other Ways

1. Double-click folder icon
2. Select folder icon, press MINUS SIGN on numeric keypad
3. Select folder to collapse, press LEFT ARROW

Copying Files to a Folder on a Floppy Disk

One common operation that every student should understand how to perform is copying a file or group of files from one disk to another disk or from one folder to another folder. On the following pages, you will create a new folder, named My Files, on the floppy disk in drive A, select a group of files in the Windows folder on drive C, and copy the files from the Windows folder on drive C to the My Files folder on drive A.

When copying files, the drive and folder containing the files to be copied are called the **source drive** and **source folder**, respectively. The drive and folder to which the files are copied are called the **destination drive** and **destination folder**, respectively. Thus, the Windows folder is the source folder, drive C is the source drive, the My Files folder is the destination folder, and drive A is the destination drive.

Creating a New Folder

In preparation for selecting and copying files from a folder on the hard drive to a folder on the floppy disk in drive A, a new folder with the name of My Files will be created on the floppy disk. Perform the following steps to create the new folder.

 To Create a New Folder

1 **Insert a formatted floppy disk into drive A on your computer.**

2 **Click the 3½ Floppy (A:) folder name in the All Folders pane and then point to an open area of the Contents pane.**

The 3½ Floppy (A:) folder name is highlighted, the contents of the 3½ Floppy (A:) folder display in the Contents pane, and the messages on the status bar change (Figure 2-11). The 3½ Floppy (A:) folder name displays in the window title and on the button in the taskbar button area. Currently, no files or folders display in the Contents pane. The files and folders may be different on your computer.

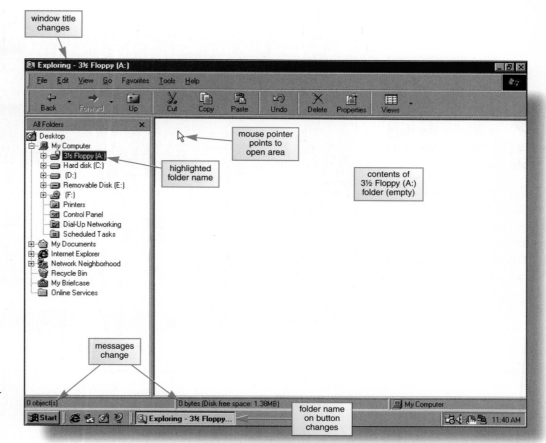

FIGURE 2-11

3 Right-click the open area of the Contents pane and then point to New on the shortcut menu.

A shortcut menu and the New submenu display. The New command is highlighted on the shortcut menu (Figure 2-12). Although no subfolders display in the Contents pane and no plus sign should precede the 3½ Floppy (A:) icon in the All Folders pane, a plus sign precedes the icon.

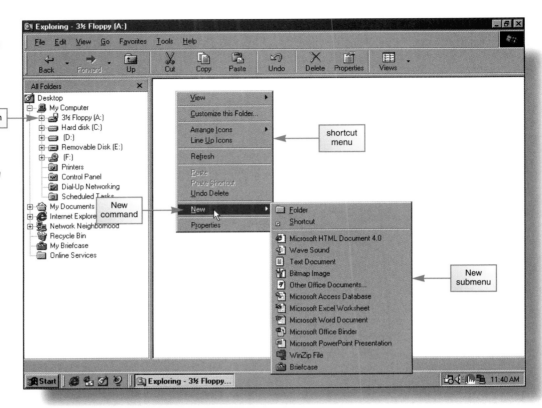

FIGURE 2-12

4 Point to Folder on the New submenu.

The Folder command is highlighted on the New submenu (Figure 2-13). Clicking the Folder command will create a folder in the Contents pane using the default folder name, New Folder.

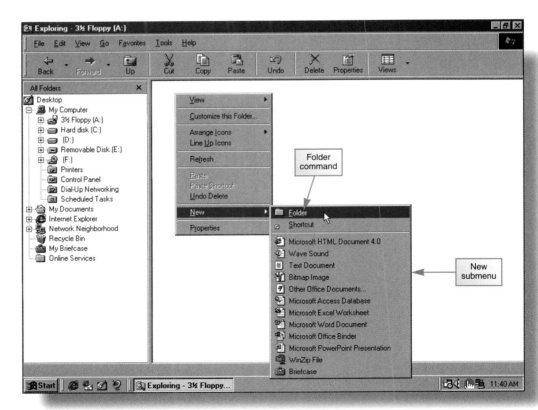

FIGURE 2-13

⑤ **Click Folder on the New submenu.**

The highlighted New Folder icon displays in the Contents pane (Figure 2-14). The text box below the icon contains the highlighted default folder name, New Folder, and an insertion point. A plus sign continues to display to the left of the 3½ Floppy (A:) icon to indicate the 3½ Floppy (A:) folder contains the New Folder subfolder. The message on the status bar indicates one object is selected in the Contents pane.

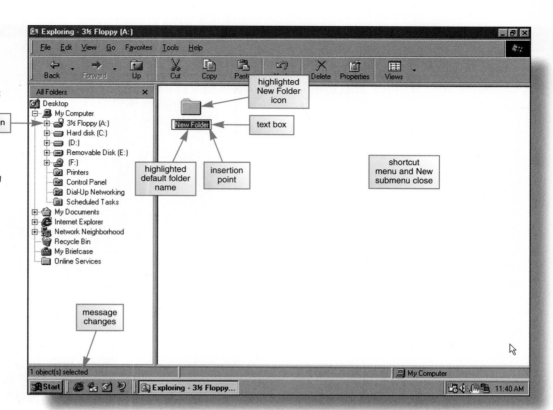

FIGURE 2-14

⑥ **Type** My Files **in the text box and then press the ENTER key.**

The new folder name, My Files, is entered and the text box is removed (Figure 2-15).

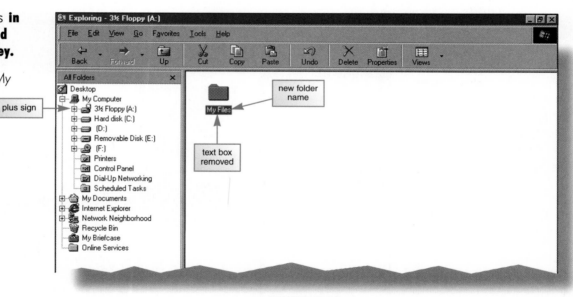

FIGURE 2-15

Other Ways

1. Select drive in All Folders pane, on File menu point to New, click Folder on New submenu

After creating the My Files folder on the floppy disk in drive A, you can save files in the folder or copy files from other folders to the folder. On the following pages, you will copy a group of files consisting of the Black Thatch, Bubbles, and Circles files from the Windows folder on drive C to the My Files folder on drive A.

Displaying the Destination Folder

To copy the three files from the Windows folder on drive C to the My Files folder on drive A, the files to be copied will be selected in the Contents pane and right-dragged to the My Files folder in the All Folders pane. Prior to selecting and right-dragging the files, the destination folder (My Files folder on drive A) must be visible in the All Folders pane, and the three files to be copied must be visible in the Contents pane.

Currently, the plus sign (+) to the left of the 3½ Floppy (A:) icon indicates the folder contains one or more subfolders that are not visible in the All Folders pane (see Figure 2-15). Perform the following steps to expand the 3½ Floppy (A:) folder to display the My Files subfolder.

TO EXPAND A FOLDER

1 Point to the plus sign to the left of the 3½ Floppy (A:) icon in the All Folders pane.

2 Click the plus sign to display the subfolders in the 3½ Floppy (A:) folder.

A minus sign replaces the plus sign preceding the 3½ Floppy (A:) folder, the folder name is highlighted, and the My Files subfolder displays in the 3½ Floppy (A:) folder, indented and aligned below the 3½ Floppy (A:) folder name (Figure 2-16).

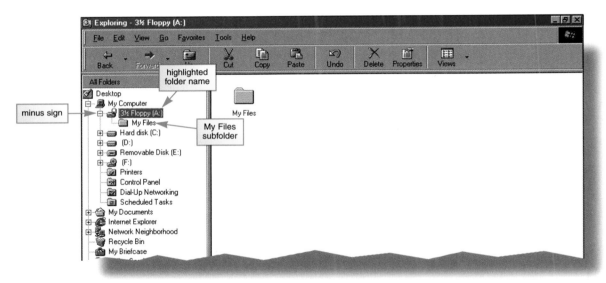

FIGURE 2-16

Displaying the Contents of the Windows Folder

Currently, the My Files folder displays in the Contents pane of the Exploring – 3½ Floppy (A:) window. To copy files from the source folder (Windows folder on drive C) to the My Files folder, the Windows folder must be visible in the All Folders pane. To make the Windows folder visible, you must expand the Hard disk (C:) folder and then click the Windows folder name to display the contents of the Windows folder in the Contents pane. Perform the steps on the next two pages to display the contents of the Windows folder.

Steps **To Display the Contents of a Folder**

1 Click the plus sign to the left of the Hard disk (C:) icon in the All Folders pane and then point to the Windows folder name.

A minus sign replaces the plus sign to the left of the Hard disk (C:) icon and the subfolders in the Hard disk (C:) folder display (Figure 2-17). In addition to folders and other files, the Windows folder contains a series of predefined graphics, called **clip art files***, that can be used with application programs.*

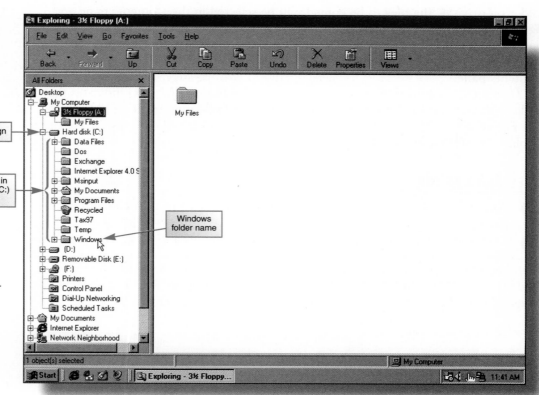

FIGURE 2-17

2 Click the Windows folder name.

The Windows folder name is highlighted in the All Folders pane, the closed folder icon to the left of the Windows folder name changes to an open folder icon, and the contents of the Windows folder display in the Contents pane (Figure 2-18).

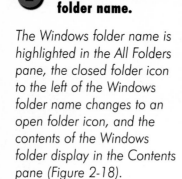

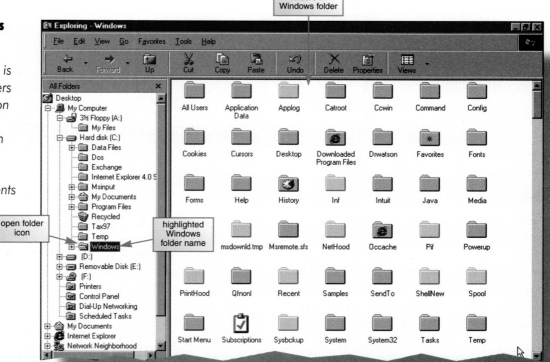

FIGURE 2-18

3 **Scroll the Contents pane to make the files in the Windows folder visible.**

The files in the Windows folder display in the Contents pane (Figure 2-19). Each file is identified by a large icon and a file name. The files in the Windows folder may be different and file extensions may display as part of the file names on your computer.

FIGURE 2-19

Changing the View

In Figure 2-19, the files in the Contents pane of the Exploring – Windows window display in Large Icons view. In **Large Icons view**, each file is represented by a large icon and a file name. Other views include Small Icons, List, and Details. List view often is useful when copying or moving files from one location to another location. In **List view**, each file is represented by a smaller icon and name, and the files are arranged in columns. Perform the following steps to change from Large Icons view to List view.

 To Change to List View

1 **Right-click an open area in the Contents pane, point to View on the shortcut menu, and then point to List on the View submenu.**

A shortcut menu displays, the View command is highlighted on the shortcut menu, the View submenu displays, and the List command is highlighted on the View submenu (Figure 2-20). A large dot to the left of the Large Icons command indicates files and folders in the Contents pane display in Large Icons view.

FIGURE 2-20

2 Click List on the View submenu.

The files and folders in the Contents pane display in List view (Figure 2-21).

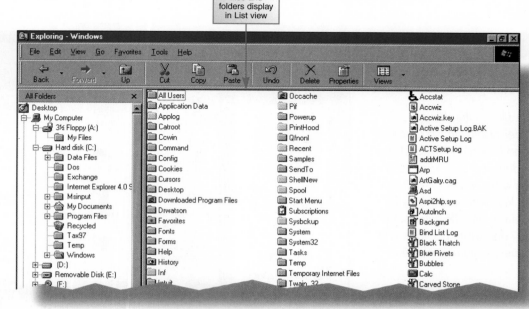

FIGURE 2-21

Other Ways

1. Click Views button on Standard Buttons toolbar repeatedly until files and folder display in List view
2. Click Views button arrow on Standard Buttons toolbar, click List
3. On View menu click List
4. Press ALT+V, press L

Selecting a Group of Files

You easily can copy a single file or group of files from one folder to another folder using Windows Explorer. To copy a single file, select the file in the Contents pane and right-drag the highlighted file to the folder in the All Folders pane where the file is to be copied. Group files are copied in a similar fashion by clicking the icon or file name of the first file in a group of files to select it. You select the remaining files in the group by pointing to each file icon or file name, holding down the CTRL key, and clicking the file icon or file name. Perform the following steps to select the group of files consisting of the Black Thatch, Bubbles, and Circles files.

To Select a Group of Files

1 Select the Black Thatch file by clicking the Black Thatch file name, and then point to the Bubbles file name.

The Black Thatch file is highlighted in the Contents pane and two messages display on the status bar (Figure 2-22). The messages indicate that one file is selected (1 object(s) selected) and the size of the file (182 bytes).

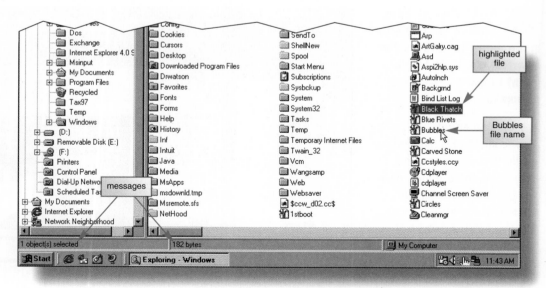

FIGURE 2-22

2 Hold down the CTRL key, click the **Bubbles** file name, release the CTRL key, and then point to the **Circles** file name.

The Black Thatch and Bubbles files are highlighted and the two messages on the status bar change to reflect the additional file selected (Figure 2-23). The messages indicate two files are selected (2 object(s) selected) and the size of the two files (2.24KB).

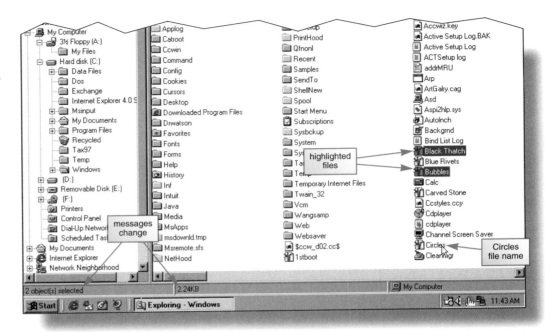

FIGURE 2-23

3 Hold down the CTRL key, click the **Circles** file name, and then release the CTRL key.

The group of files consisting of the Black Thatch, Bubbles, and Circles files is highlighted and the messages on the status bar change to reflect the selection of a third file (Figure 2-24). The messages indicate three files are selected (3 object(s) selected) and the size of the three files (2.43KB).

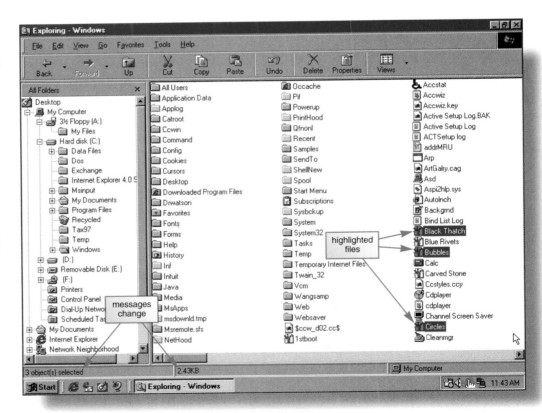

FIGURE 2-24

Other Ways

1. To select contiguous files, select first file name, hold down SHIFT key, click last file name

2. To select all files, on Edit menu click Select All

Copying a Group of Files

After selecting a group of files, copy the files to the My Files folder on drive A by pointing to any highlighted file name in the Contents pane and right-dragging the file name to the My Files folder in the All Folders pane. Perform the following steps to copy a group of files.

 To Copy a Group of Files

1 If necessary, scroll the All Folders pane to make the My Files folder visible. Point to the highlighted Black Thatch file name in the Contents pane.

The pointer points to the highlighted Black Thatch file name in the Contents pane and the My Files folder is visible in the All Folders pane (Figure 2-25).

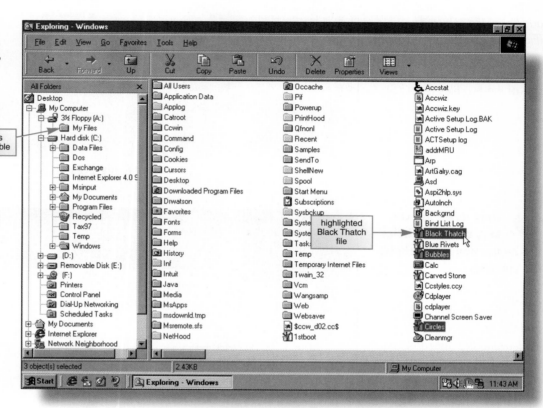

FIGURE 2-25

2 Right-drag the Black Thatch file over the My Files folder name in the All Folders pane.

As you drag the file, an outline of three icons and three horizontal lines displays and the My Files folder name is highlighted (Figure 2-26). The mouse pointer contains a plus sign to indicate the group of files is being copied, not moved.

FIGURE 2-26

3 **Release the right mouse button and then point to Copy Here on the shortcut menu.**

A shortcut menu displays and the Copy Here command on the shortcut menu is highlighted (Figure 2-27).

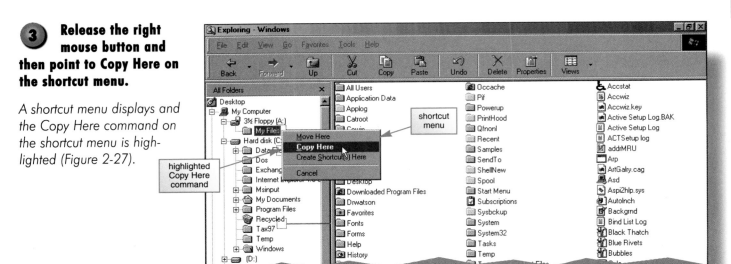

FIGURE 2-27

4 **Click Copy Here.**

The Copying dialog box displays and remains on the screen while each file is copied to the My Files folder (Figure 2-28). The Copying dialog box shown in Figure 2-28 indicates the Black Thatch.bmp file is being copied.

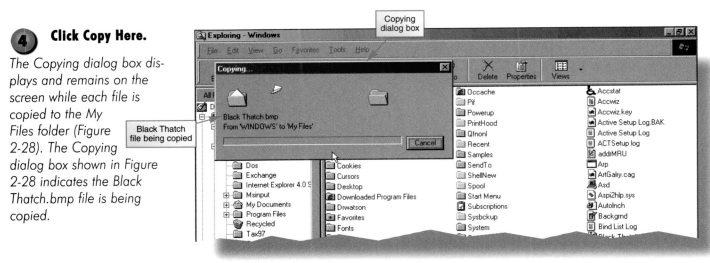

FIGURE 2-28

Displaying the Contents of the My Files Folder

After copying a group of files, you should verify the files were copied into the correct folder. To view the files that were copied to the My Files folder, perform the following steps.

TO DISPLAY THE CONTENTS OF A FOLDER

1 Point to the My Files folder name in the All Folders pane.

2 Click the My Files folder name.

The highlighted My Files folder name displays in the All Folders pane, the open folder icon replaces the closed folder icon to the left of the My Files folder name, the contents of the My Files folder display in the Contents pane, and the message on the status bar changes (Figure 2-29 on the next page). The status bar message indicates 1.38MB of free disk space on the disk in drive A.

Other Ways

1. Drag file to copy from Contents pane to folder icon in All Folder pane

2. Select file to copy in Contents pane, click Copy button on Standard Buttons toolbar, select folder icon to receive copy, click Paste button on Standard Buttons toolbar

3. Select file to copy in Contents pane, on Edit menu click Copy, select folder icon to receive copy, on Edit menu click Paste

4. Select file to copy, press CTRL+C, select folder icon to receive copy, press CTRL+V

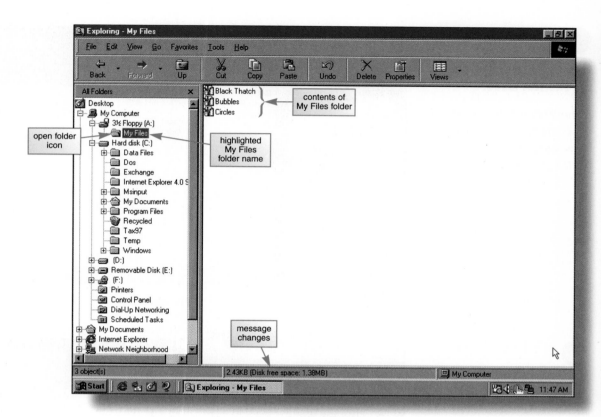

FIGURE 2-29

Renaming a File or Folder

For various reasons, you may wish to change the name of a file or folder on disk. Perform the following steps to change the name of the Circles file on drive A to Blue Circles.

 To Rename a File

1 **Point to the Circles file name in the Contents pane (Figure 2-30).**

The mouse pointer points to the Circles file name.

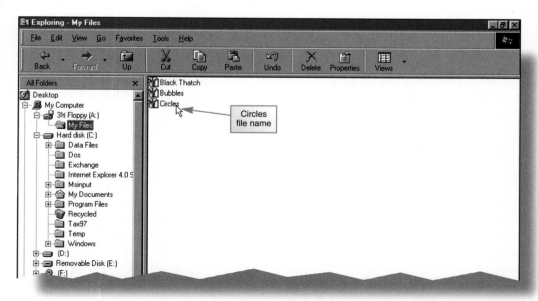

FIGURE 2-30

2 **Click the Circles file name twice (do not double-click the file name).**

A text box containing the highlighted Circles file name and insertion point displays (Figure 2-31).

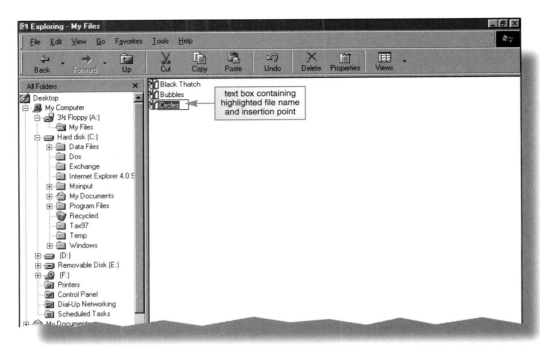

FIGURE 2-31

3 **Type** Blue Circles **and then press the ENTER key.**

The file name changes to Blue Circles and the text box surrounding the file name is removed (Figure 2-32).

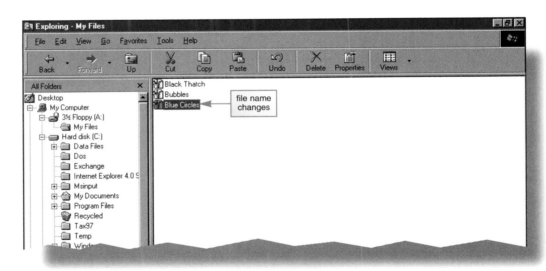

FIGURE 2-32

Follow the same procedure to change a folder name. The steps on the next page change the name of the My Files folder to Clip Art Files.

Other Ways

1. Right-click file name in Contents pane, click Rename on shortcut menu, type new name, press ENTER

2. Select file name in Contents pane, on File menu click Rename, type new name, press ENTER

3. Select file name in Contents pane, press F2, type new name, press ENTER

4. Select file name, press ALT+F, press M, type new name, press ENTER

Steps | To Rename a Folder

1 **Point to the My Files folder name in the All Folders pane (Figure 2-33).**

The mouse pointer points to the My Files folder name.

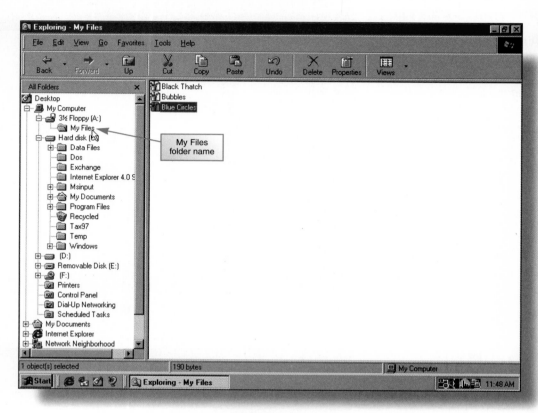

FIGURE 2-33

2 **Click the My Files folder name twice (do not double-click the folder name).**

A text box containing the highlighted My Files name and insertion point displays (Figure 2-34).

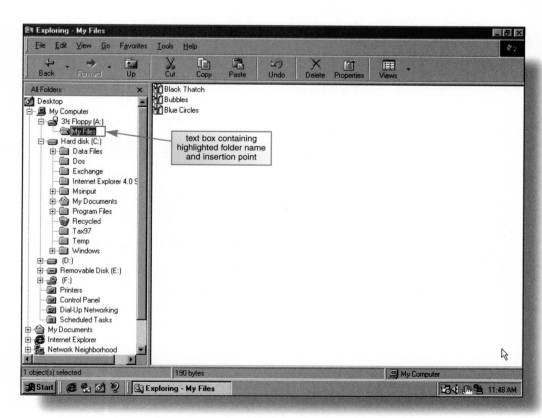

FIGURE 2-34

3 **Type** Clip Art
Files **and then
press the ENTER key.**

*The folder name changes to
Clip Art Files and the text box
surrounding the folder name
is removed (Figure 2-35). The
new folder name replaces the
old folder name in the window title and on the button in
the taskbar button area.*

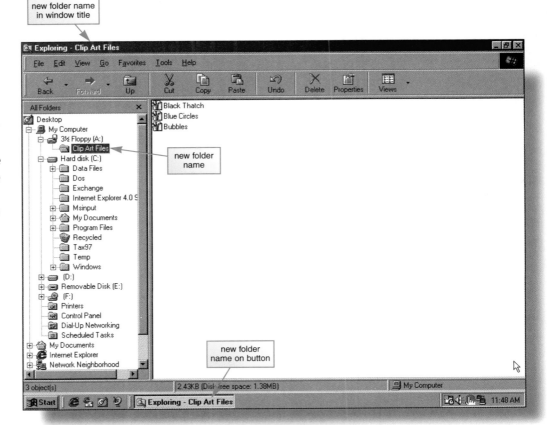

FIGURE 2-35

Deleting a File or Folder

When you no longer need a file or folder, you can delete it. Two methods commonly
are used to delete a file or folder. One method uses the Delete command on the
shortcut menu that displays when you right-click the file name or folder name.
Another method involves right-dragging the unneeded file or folder to the Recycle
Bin. The Recycle Bin icon is located at the left edge of the desktop (see Figure 2-1 on
page WIN 2.5).

When you delete a file or folder on the hard drive using the Recycle Bin,
Windows 98 temporarily stores the deleted file or folder in the Recycle Bin until you
permanently discard the contents of the Recycle Bin by emptying the Recycle Bin.
Until the Recycle Bin is emptied, you can retrieve the files and folders you have
deleted previously by mistake or other reasons. Unlike deleting files or folders on the
hard drive, when you delete a file or folder located on a floppy disk, the file or folder
is deleted immediately and not stored in the Recycle Bin.

On the following pages, you will delete the Bubbles and Black Thatch files. The
Bubbles file will be deleted by right-clicking. The Black Thatch file will be deleted by
right-dragging the file to the Recycle Bin.

Deleting a File by Right-Clicking Its File Name

Right-clicking a file name produces a shortcut menu that contains the Delete
command. To illustrate how to delete a file by right-clicking, perform the steps on
the next two pages to delete the Bubbles file.

Other Ways

1. Right-click folder name in
   Contents pane, click Rename
   on shortcut menu, type new
   name, press ENTER

2. Select folder name in
   Contents pane, on File menu
   click Rename, type new
   name, press ENTER

3. Select folder name in
   Contents pane, press F2,
   type new name, press ENTER

4. Select folder name, press
   ALT+F, press M, type new
   name, press ENTER

To Delete a File by Right-Clicking

1 **Right-click the Bubbles file name in the Contents pane and then point to the Delete command on the shortcut menu.**

A shortcut menu displays and the Bubbles file name is highlighted (Figure 2-36).

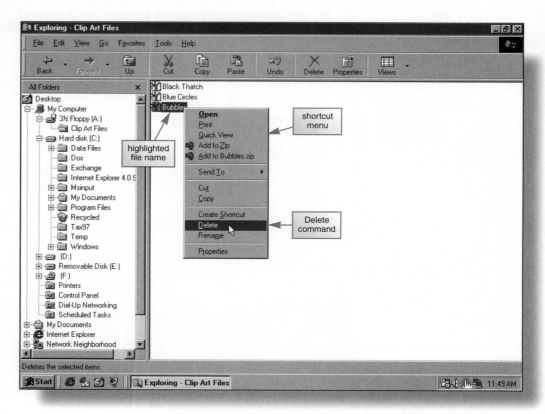

FIGURE 2-36

2 **Click Delete. When the Confirm File Delete dialog box displays, point to the Yes button.**

The Confirm File Delete dialog box displays (Figure 2-37). The dialog box contains the message, Are you sure you want to delete 'Bubbles'?, and the Yes and No command buttons.

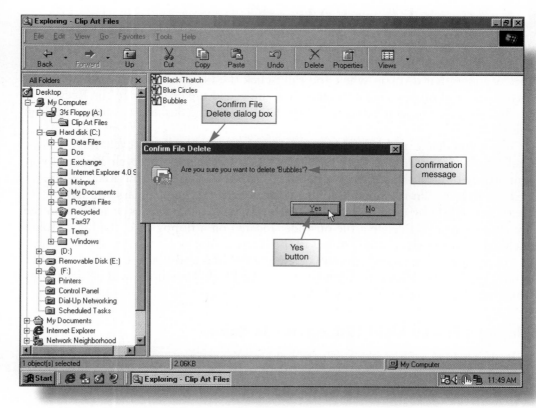

FIGURE 2-37

3 **Click the Yes button.**

A Deleting dialog box displays while the file is being deleted, and then the Bubbles file is removed from the Contents pane (Figure 2-38).

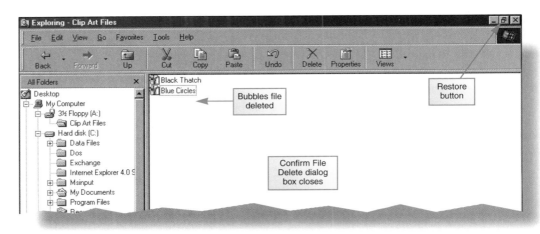

FIGURE 2-38

Deleting a File by Right-Dragging Its File Name

Another method to delete a file is to right-drag the file name from the Contents pane of the window to the Recycle Bin icon on the desktop. Right-dragging produces a shortcut menu that contains the Move Here command. Currently, the Exploring – Clip Art Files window is maximized and occupies the entire desktop. With a maximized window, you cannot right-drag a file to the Recycle Bin. To allow you to right-drag a file, you first must restore the Exploring – Clip Art Files window to its original size by clicking the Restore button on the title bar. Perform the following steps to delete the Black Thatch file by right-dragging its file name.

Other Ways

1. Click file name, click Delete button on Standard Buttons toolbar, click Yes button
2. Click file name, press DELETE, press Y

 **To Delete a File by Right-Dragging**

1 **Click the Restore button on the Exploring – Clip Art Files window title bar and then point to the Black Thatch file name in the Contents pane.**

The Exploring – Clip Art Files window is restored to its original size before maximizing and the Maximize button replaces the Restore button on the title bar (Figure 2-39).

FIGURE 2-39

2 Right-drag the Black Thatch file name over the Recycle Bin icon and then point to the Move Here command on the shortcut menu.

A shortcut menu displays and the Move Here command is highlighted (Figure 2-40). The Black Thatch file name displays on top of the Recycle Bin icon on the desktop.

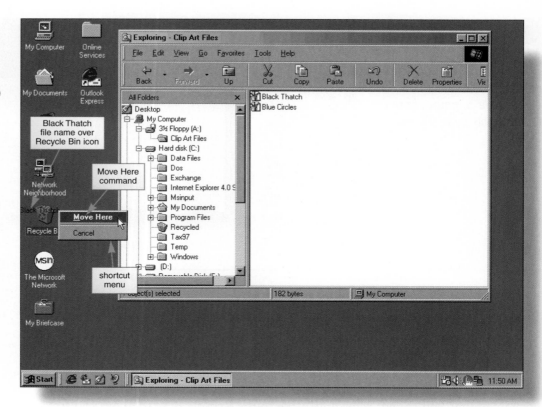

FIGURE 2-40

3 Click Move Here. When the Confirm File Delete dialog box displays, point to the Yes button.

The Confirm File Delete dialog box displays (Figure 2-41). The dialog box contains the message, Are you sure you want to delete 'Black Thatch'?, and the Yes and No command buttons.

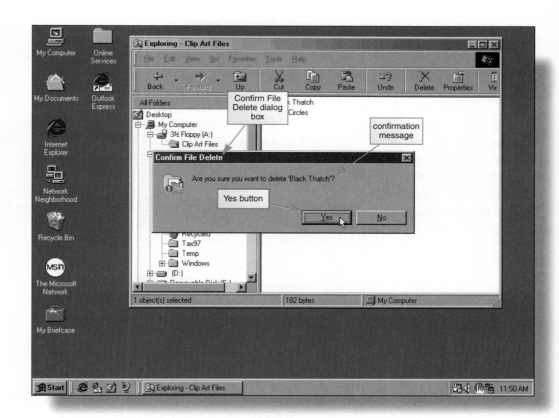

FIGURE 2-41

4 Click the Yes button.

A Deleting dialog box displays while the file is being deleted, and then the Black Thatch file is removed from the Contents pane (Figure 2-42).

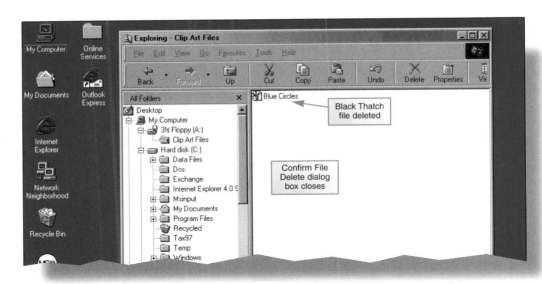

FIGURE 2-42

Whether you delete a file by right-clicking or right-dragging, you can use the file selection techniques illustrated earlier in this project to delete a group of files. When deleting a group of files, click the Yes button in the Confirm Multiple File Delete dialog box to confirm the deletion of the group of files.

Deleting a Folder

When you delete a folder, Windows 98 deletes any files or subfolders in the folder. You can delete a folder using the two methods shown earlier to delete files (right-clicking or right-dragging). Perform the following steps to delete the Clip Art Files folder on drive A by right-dragging the folder to the Recycle Bin.

 To Delete a Folder

1 Point to the Clip Art Files folder name in the All Folders pane (Figure 2-43).

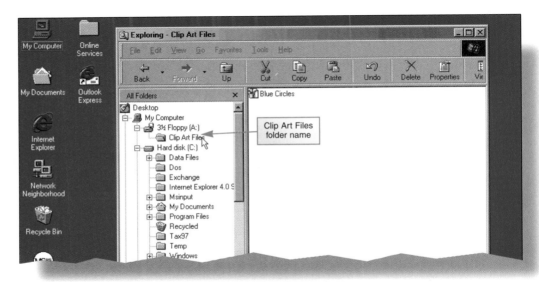

FIGURE 2-43

2 Right-drag the Clip Art Files icon to the Recycle Bin icon and then point to Move Here on the shortcut menu.

A shortcut menu displays (Figure 2-44).

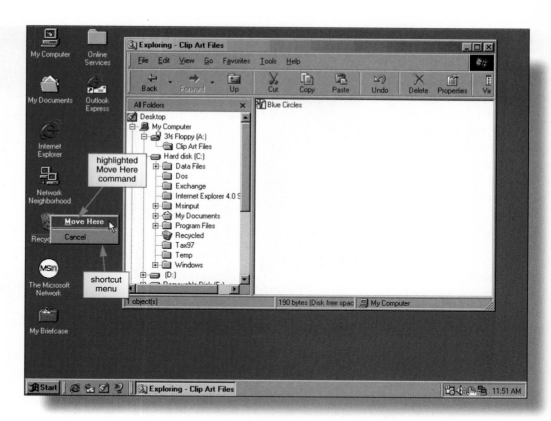

FIGURE 2-44

3 Click Move Here. When the Confirm Folder Delete dialog box displays, point to the Yes button.

The Confirm Folder Delete dialog box displays (Figure 2-45). The dialog box contains the message, Are you sure you want to remove the folder 'Clip Art Files' and all its contents?, and the Yes and No command buttons.

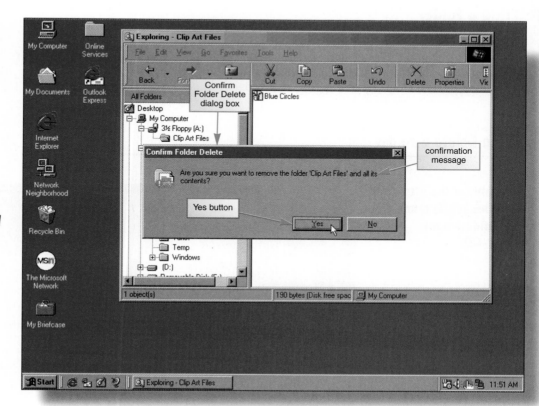

FIGURE 2-45

4 Click the Yes button.

A Deleting dialog box displays while the folder is being deleted, the Clip Art Files folder is removed from the All Folders pane, and a plus sign replaces the minus sign preceding the 3½ Floppy (A:) icon (Figure 2-46).

5 Remove the floppy disk from drive A.

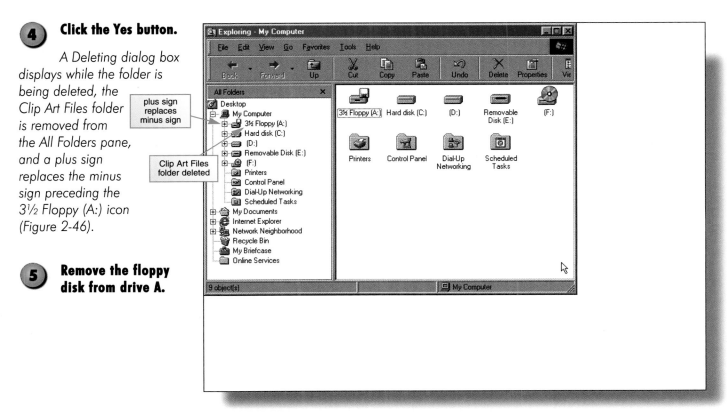

FIGURE 2-46

Other Ways

1. Click folder, click Delete button on Standard Buttons toolbar, click Yes button
2. Click folder, press DELETE, press Y

Quitting Windows Explorer and Shutting Down Windows 98

After completing your work with Windows Explorer, you should quit Windows Explorer and then shut down Windows.

Perform the following steps to quit Windows Explorer.

TO QUIT AN APPLICATION

1 Point to the Close button in the Exploring window.

2 Click the Close button.

Windows 98 closes the Windows Explorer window and quits Windows Explorer.

Perform the following steps to shut down Windows 98.

TO SHUT DOWN WINDOWS 98

1 Click the Start button on the taskbar.

2 Click Shut Down on the Start menu.

3 Click the OK button in the Shut Down Windows dialog box.

4 Turn off the computer.

Project Summary

In this project, you used Windows Explorer to select and copy a group of files, change views, display the contents of a folder, create a folder, expand and collapse a folder, and rename and delete a file and a folder.

What You Should Know

Having completed this project, you now should be able to perform the following tasks:

▶ Change to List View *(WIN 2.17)*

▶ Collapse a Folder *(WIN 2.11)*

▶ Copy a Group of Files *(WIN 2.20)*

▶ Create a New Folder *(WIN 2.12)*

▶ Delete a File by Right-Clicking *(WIN 2.26)*

▶ Delete a File by Right-Dragging *(WIN 2.27)*

▶ Delete a Folder *(WIN 2.29)*

▶ Display the Contents of a Folder (WIN 2.9, WIN 2.16, WIN 2.21)

▶ Expand a Folder (WIN 2.10, WIN 2.15)

▶ Quit an Application *(WIN 2.31)*

▶ Rename a File *(WIN 2.22)*

▶ Rename a Folder *(WIN 2.24)*

▶ Select a Group of Files *(WIN 2.18)*

▶ Shut Down Windows 98 *(WIN 2.31)*

▶ Start Windows Explorer and Maximize Its Window *(WIN 2.6)*

Test Your Knowledge

1 True/False

Instructions: Circle T if the statement is true or F if the statement is false.

T F   1. Windows Explorer is an application you can use to organize and work with the files and folders on the computer.

T F   2. Double-clicking the My Computer icon is the best way to open Windows Explorer.

T F   3. The contents of the highlighted folder in the All Folders pane displays in the Contents pane.

T F   4. To display the contents of drive C on your computer in the Contents pane, click the plus sign in the small box next to the drive C icon.

T F   5. A folder that is contained within another folder is called a subfolder.

T F   6. To display the contents of a folder, right-click its folder name.

T F   7. Collapsing a folder removes the subfolders from the hierarchy of folders in the All Folders pane.

T F   8. After you expand a drive or folder, the information in the Contents pane is always the same as the information displayed below the drive or folder icon in the All Folders pane.

T F   9. The source folder is the folder containing the files to be copied.

T F   10. You select a group of files in the Contents pane by pointing to each icon or file name and clicking the mouse button.

2 Multiple Choice

Instructions: Circle the correct response.

1. The All Folder pane in the Exploring - My Computer window contains the _____.
   a. hierarchy of folders
   b. source folder
   c. source drive
   d. contents of the highlighted folder in the Contents pane

2. The _____ contains the Desktop icon.
   a. Contents pane
   b. status bar
   c. All Folders pane
   d. Standard Buttons toolbar

3. To display the contents of a folder in the Contents pane, _____.
   a. double-click the plus sign next to the folder icon
   b. right-click the folder icon in the All Folders pane
   c. click the folder icon in the Contents pane
   d. click the folder icon in the All Folders pane

(continued)

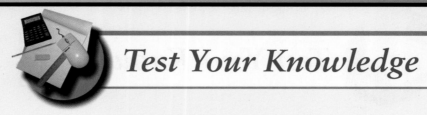

Test Your Knowledge

Multiple Choice *(continued)*

4. You _____ the minus sign preceding a folder icon to expand a folder.
   a. click
   b. drag
   c. double-click
   d. point to

5. When an expanded file is collapsed in the All Folders pane, _____.
   a. the expansion closes and the contents of the folder display in the Contents pane
   b. the entire Exploring - My Computer window closes
   c. the computer beeps at you because you cannot perform this activity
   d. the My Computer window displays

6. To select multiple files in the Contents pane, _____.
   a. right-click each file icon
   b. hold down the shift key and then click each file icon you want to select
   c. hold down the ctrl key and then click each file icon you want to select
   d. hold down the ctrl key and then double-click each file icon you want to select

7. After selecting a group of files, you _____ the group to copy the files to a new folder.
   a. click
   b. right-drag
   c. double-click
   d. none of the above

8. In _____ view, each file or folder in the Contents pane is represented by a smaller icon, and the files or folders are arranged in columns.
   a. Large Icons
   b. Small Icons
   c. List
   d. Details

9. A file or folder can be renamed by _____.
   a. right-dragging its file name
   b. double-clicking its file name
   c. dragging its file name
   d. clicking its file name twice

10. A file can be deleted by right-dragging the file name from the Contents pane of the window to the _____ icon on the desktop.
    a. My Computer
    b. Network Neighborhood
    c. Recycle Bin
    d. My Briefcase

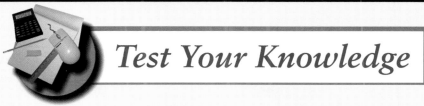

Test Your Knowledge

3 Understanding the Exploring - My Computer Window

Instructions: In Figure 2-47 arrows point to several items in the Exploring - My Computer window. Identify the items or objects in the spaces provided.

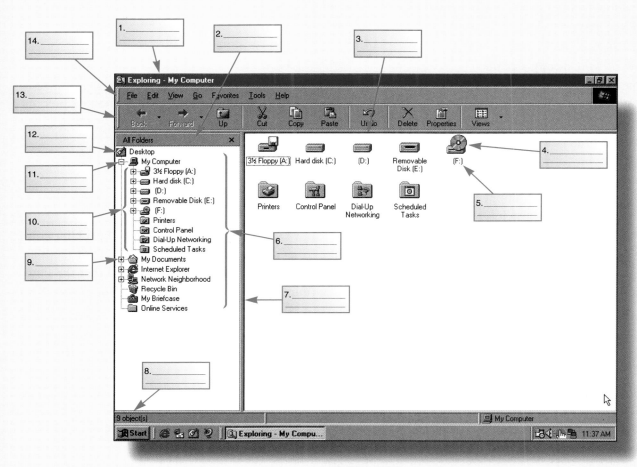

FIGURE 2-47

Use Help

1 Using Windows Help

Instructions: Use Windows Help and a computer to perform the following tasks.

1. If necessary, start Microsoft Windows 98.
2. Use Windows Help to answer the following questions about paths.
   a. What is a path? _____
   b. What does a path include? _____
   c. How do you specify a path? _____
   d. What do you do if your file name contains more than eight characters? _____
3. In the Windows Help window, click the Index tab if necessary. Type windows explorer in the text box and then answer the following questions about Windows Explorer.
   a. How do you create a folder in Windows Explorer? _____
   b. How do you copy a disk in Windows Explorer? _____
   c. How do you display the full path of a file in the title bar? _____
   d. How do you print an unopened file from Windows Explorer? _____
   e. How can you cause Explorer to start each time you start Windows 98? _____
4. After typing and saving a memo in which you explained CD-ROM drives to your manager, Lori Hill, you now want to recall other topics you covered in the memo. You can remember neither the name of the file nor where you stored it on your computer. You read something in your Windows 98 manual that the Find command could be used to find lost files. Using Help, determine what you must do to find your letter. Write those steps in the spaces provided.

   _____
   _____
   _____
5. You and a friend both recently bought computers. She was lucky and received a color printer as her birthday gift. You would like to print some of your more colorful documents on her color printer. For a cost your budgets can handle, you and your friend can buy a network card and some cable and hook up your computers on a network. Then, you can print documents stored on your computer on her color printer. Using Windows Help, determine if you can share her printer. If so, what must you do in Windows 98 to make this become a reality. Print the Help pages that document your answer.
6. You hardly can believe that last week you won a laptop computer at a charity dance. The application programs on the laptop are the same as those on your desktop computer. The only trouble is that when you use your laptop computer to modify a file, you would like the same file on your desktop to be modified also. In that way, you can work on the file either on your desktop computer or on your laptop computer. A friend mentioned that the My Briefcase feature of Windows 98 allows you to do what you want to do. Using Windows Help, find out all you can about My Briefcase. Print the Help pages that specify how to keep files on both your desktop and laptop computers synchronized with each other.

1 File and Program Properties

Instructions: Use a computer to perform the following tasks and answer the questions.

1. If necessary, start Microsoft Windows 98.
2. Right-click the My Computer icon on the desktop and click Explore on the shortcut menu.
3. Click the plus sign in the small box to the left of the drive C icon in the All Folders pane on your computer.
4. Scroll the All Folders pane until the Windows icon is visible and then click the Windows icon.
5. Scroll the Contents pane until the Black Thatch icon is visible. If the Black Thatch icon does not display on your computer, find another Paint icon.
6. Right-click the Black Thatch icon and then click Properties on the shortcut menu.
7. Answer the following questions about the Black Thatch file:
   a. What type of file is Black Thatch? _____
   b. What is the path for the location of the Black Thatch file? _____
   c. What is the size (in bytes) of the Black Thatch file? _____
   d. What is the MS-DOS name of the Black Thatch file? _____ The tilde (~) charac-
      ter is placed in the MS-DOS file name when the Windows 98 file name is greater than eight characters.
      Windows 98 uses the first six characters of the long file name, the tilde character, and a number to dis-
      tinguish the file from other files that might have the same first six characters.
   e. When was the file created? _____
   f. When was the file last modified? _____
   g. When was the file last accessed? _____
8. Click the Cancel button in the Black Thatch Properties dialog box.
9. Scroll the Contents pane to display the Notepad icon.
10. Right-click the Notepad icon and then click Properties on the shortcut menu.
11. Answer the following questions:
   a. What type of file is Notepad? _____
   b. What is the path of the Notepad file? _____
   c. What is the size (in bytes) of the Notepad file? _____
   d. What is the file extension of the Notepad file? What does it stand for? _____
   e. What is the file version of the Notepad file? _____
   f. What is the file's description? _____
   g. Who is the copyright owner of Notepad? _____
   h. For what language is Notepad written? _____
12. Click the Cancel button in the Notepad Properties dialog box.
13. Close all open windows.

In the Lab

2 Windows Explorer

Instructions: Use a computer to perform the following tasks.

1. Start Microsoft Windows 98 and connect to the Internet.
2. Right-click the Start button on the taskbar, click Explore on the shortcut menu, and maximize the Exploring - Start Menu window.
3. If necessary, scroll to the left in the All Folders pane so the Start Menu and Programs icons are visible.
4. Click the plus sign in the small box to the left of the Programs icon.
5. Click the Internet Explorer icon in the Programs folder in the All Folders pane.
6. Double-click the Internet Explorer icon in the Contents pane to launch the Internet Explorer application. What is the URL of the Web page that displays in the Address bar in the Microsoft Internet Explorer window? _____
7. Click the URL in the Address bar of the Internet Explorer window to select it. Type www.scsite.com and then press the ENTER key.
8. Scroll the Web page to display the Shelly Cashman Series textbook titles.
9. Click the textbook title of your Windows 98 textbook.
10. Right-click the Space Needle clip art image on the Web page, click Save Picture As on the shortcut menu, and click the Save button in the Save Picture dialog box to save the image in the My Documents folder.
11. Click the Close button in the Microsoft Internet Explorer window.
12. Scroll to the top of the All Folders pane to make the drive C icon visible.
13. Click the minus sign in the box to the left of the drive C icon. The 3½ Floppy (A:) and My Documents icons should be visible.
14. Click the My Documents folder.
15. Right-click the Space Needle icon and then click Properties on the shortcut menu.
    a. What type of file is the Space Needle file? _____
    b. When was the file last modified? _____
    c. What is the size of the file? _____
16. Click the Cancel button in the Space Needle Properties dialog box.
17. Insert a formatted floppy disk in drive A of your computer.
18. Right-drag the Space Needle icon over the 3½ Floppy (A:) icon in the All Folder pane. Click Move Here on the shortcut menu. Click the 3½ Floppy (A:) icon in the All Folders pane. Is the Space Needle file stored on drive A? _____
19. Click the Close button in the Exploring - 3½ Floppy (A:) window.

In the Lab

3 Window Toolbars

Instructions: Use a computer to perform the following tasks.

1. If necessary, start Microsoft Windows 98.
2. Right-click the My Computer icon on the desktop and then click Explore on the shortcut menu.
3. Expand the drive C icon in the All Folders pane on your computer.
4. Scroll the All Folders pane until the Windows icon is visible and then click the Windows icon.
5. Click View on the menu bar and then click List.
6. Click View on the menu bar and then point to Toolbars. If a check mark does not display to the left of the Address Bar command on the Toolbars submenu, click Adderss Bar. The Address bar displays in the My Computer window.
7. Click the list box arrow containing C:\WINDOWS entry.
8. Click Control Panel in the list box. How did the window change? _____
9. Double-click the Windows icon in the All Folders pane. What happened? _____
10. Scroll the Contents pane if necessary to display the Blue Rivets icon. If the Blue Rivets icon does not display on your computer, find another Paint icon. Click the Blue Rivets icon and then point to the Copy button on the Standard Buttons toolbar.
11. Click the Copy button. Do you see any change? If so, what? _____
12. Insert a formatted floppy disk in drive A of your computer.
13. Click the list box arrow containing the C:\WINDOWS entry.
14. Click the 3½ Floppy (A:) icon in the list box. What happened? _____
15. Click the Paste button on the Standard Buttons toolbar. The Blue Rivets icon displays in the 3½ Floppy (A:) window.
16. Click the Blue Rivets icon to highlight the icon, click the Delete button on the Standard Buttons toolbar, and then click the Yes button in the Confirm File Delete dialog box.
17. In the 3½ Floppy (A:) window, return the toolbar status to what it was prior to step 6.
18. Click View on the menu bar and then click Large Icons.
19. Close the 3½ Floppy (A:) window.

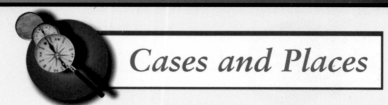

Cases and Places

The difficulty of these case studies varies:
▌ are the least difficult; ▌▌ are more difficult; and ▌▌▌ are the most difficult.

1 ▌ A key feature of Windows 98 is the capability of modifying the view of a window to suit individual preferences and needs. Using Windows Explorer, display the Hard disk (C:) folder in the Contents pane and then experiment with the different commands on the View menu. Describe the effects of the Large Icons, Small Icons, List, and Details commands on the icons in the Contents pane. When using Details view, explain how clicking one of the buttons at the top of the Contents pane (such as Name or Type) changes the window. Try out diverse arrangements of icons on the Contents pane by pointing to the Arrange Icons command on the View menu and then clicking various commands on the Arrange Icons submenu. Finally, specify situations in which you think some of the views you have seen would be most appropriate.

2 ▌ When the Hard disk (C:) folder is displayed in the Contents pane of the Exploring window, it is clear that an enormous number of folders and files are stored on your computer's hard disk. Imagine how hard it would be to search through all the folders and files manually to locate a specific file. Windows 98 provides the Find command to perform a quick search for you. Click Tools on the Exploring window menu bar, point to Find, and then click Files or Folders on the Find submenu. Learn about each sheet in the Find: All Files window by clicking a tab (Name & Location, Date, or Advanced), clicking the Help menu, clicking What's This? on the Help menu, and then clicking an item in the dialog box. Try finding a file using each sheet. Finally, explain how the Find command is used and describe a circumstance in which each sheet would be useful. When you are finished, click the Close button on the window title bar to close the Find: All Files window.

3 ▌ Backing up files is an important way to protect data and ensure it is not lost or destroyed accidentally. File backup on a personal computer can use a variety of devices and techniques. Using the Internet, a library, personal computer magazines, or other resources, determine the types of devices used to store backed up data, the schedules, methods, and techniques for backing up data, and the consequences of not backing up data. Write a brief report of your findings.

4 ▌▌ A hard disk must be maintained to be used most efficiently. This maintenance includes deleting old files, defragmenting a disk so it does not waste space, and from time to time finding and attempting to correct disk failures. Using the Internet, a library, Windows 98 Help, or other research facilities, determine the maintenance that should be performed on hard disks, including the type of maintenance, when it should be performed, how long it takes to perform the maintenance, and the risks, if any, of not performing the maintenance. Write a brief report on the information you obtain.

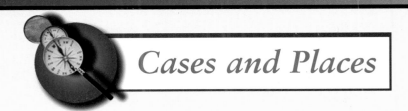

Cases and Places

5 ▶▶ The quest for more and faster disk storage continues as application programs grow larger and create sound and graphics files. One technique for increasing the amount of data that can be stored on a disk is disk compression. Disk compression programs, using a variety of mathematical algorithms, store data in less space on a hard disk. Many companies sell software you can load on your computer to perform the task. Windows 98 has disk compression capabilities as part of the operating system. Visit a computer store and find two disk compression programs you can buy. Write a brief report comparing the two packages to the disk compression capabilities of Windows 98. Discuss the similarities and differences between the programs and identify the program that claims to be the most efficient in compressing data.

6 ▶▶▶ Some individuals in the computer industry think the Windows operating system is deficient when it comes to ease of file management. Therefore, they have developed and marketed software that augments the operating systems to provide different and, they claim, improved services for file management. Visit a computer store and inquire about products such as Symantec's Norton Navigator for Windows 98. Write a brief report comparing the products you tested with Windows 98. Explain which you prefer and why.

7 ▶▶▶ Data stored on disk is one of a company's more valuable assets. If that data were to be stolen, lost, or compromised so it could not be accessed, the company literally could go out of business. Therefore, companies go to great lengths to protect their data. Visit a company or business in your area. Find out how it protects its data against viruses, unauthorized access, and even against such natural disasters as fire and tornadoes. Prepare a brief report that describes the procedures. In your report, point out any areas where you see the company has not adequately protected its data.

Index